WRITINGS FROM
THE ONE

~ 108 Insights From The Divine ~

The Experiential Guide to
THE FIELD of Grace through Deeksha

JULIA DESMOND

BALBOA.
PRESS

A DIVISION OF HAY HOUSE

Balboa Press books may be ordered through booksellers or by contacting:

Balboa Press
A Division of Hay House
1663 Liberty Drive
Bloomington, IN 47403
www.balboapress.com
1-(877) 407-4847

ISBN: 978-1-4525-5536-2 (sc)
ISBN: 978-1-4525-5538-6 (hc)
ISBN: 978-1-4525-5537-9 (e)

Library of Congress Control Number: 2012913580

Printed in the United States of America

Balboa Press rev. date: 11/30/2012

CONTENTS

INTRODUCTION

Julia Desmond spent her childhood in the Midwestern United States, growing up in the countryside of Wisconsin with her four older brothers.

She found she loved to travel the world when she was 18 and spent 6 months in Africa teaching English in a remote village of Kenya. And while her affinity for numbers led her to a career in Investment Banking, she still continued to learn about other people and cultures by traveling overseas when she could, particularly to India and throughout Asia.

After leaving the Investment Business in her thirties, Julia immersed herself in spiritual traditions from all over the world, and found DEEKSHA originating from India as a very accelerated path for Awakening. Julia Desmond is currently a Oneness Trainer in Colorado and lives with her husband in the Aspen area.

Julia is a world citizen, open to all paths, all beliefs, all faiths, and all teachings. She derives her own truth from her experiences and realizations. It is her wish to help humanity at this time by sharing these simple Insights from her Divine, in the sincere hope that they will lead to other's experiencing their own Insights from their personal Divine.

These 108 Insights can be applied universally to the journey of Awakening.

Julia invites you to take this journey now through the "Writings from the ONE". This book is intended to be a readily accessible "handbook of Grace". You can pick it up at any time and read one of the topics and Insights. You will realize that Awakening is one of the most important roles on the planet at this time. The words of Grace are meant to be shared with anyone who is ready to Awaken, so please feel free to share them ~ The Deeksha energy is transferred through these words of Grace, activating and initiating Awakening ~

At the back of this book is an Addendum Section explaining in detail information about the Oneness University in India. The Oneness University is a small spiritual school utilizing Deeksha and Oneness Processes for Awakening and God-Realization. Some helpful websites are: www.OnenessUniversity.org and www.AspenDeeksha.com.

PART 1

1

GRACE IS THE MISSING LINK TO ACCESS THE UNIVERSAL SPIRITUAL LAWS ~

Grace is the energetic tool to unlock the mysteries of the Universe. "NO"-thing happens without Grace. Grace is the energetic "field," a.k.a. *THE FIELD of Grace* ~ It propels us as humans and propels all life in this Universe ~ When one has access to Grace, unlimited amounts of Grace, anything can happen ~

There is a tool on the planet right now to *harness this Grace,* in concentrated intention, to literally be "gifted" to others ~ *A Divine gift to fuel a person's life in a very accelerated way* ~

This tool is known as *Deeksha,* which is the Sanskrit word meaning "benediction." This energy transfer of Deeksha is equal to the benediction of Grace ~

~ Deeksha is this energetic tool of Grace ~

And this tool is at the fingertips of hundreds of thousands of individuals all across the planet, in every nation, from every background, from varied religious and spiritual sectors ~ the givers of Deeksha, a.k.a. "Deeksha Givers," are clear vehicles to transfer this Grace through their hands, through their intention, and some through their eyes.

We live in such a timeframe right now; a twenty-six-thousand-year cycle within our Universe is ending and beginning in this year of 2012. So what does this mean for the modern man living in everyday society: with families, bills, and responsibilities to keep up with?

IT MEANS:

THERE IS A SHIFT HAPPENING ~

A SHIFT IN PERCEPTION ~

A SHIFT IN CONSCIOUSNESS ~

A SHIFT IN THE "INNER WORLD" ~

WHICH ULTIMATELY BRINGS A SHIFT IN THE OUTER WORLD ~

This ancient energetic tool of Deeksha has been on the planet for thousands of years, and is resurfacing right now, throughout the planet, on a grand scale, to help facilitate this shift ~

~ THIS SHIFT OF AWAKENING ~

2

THE UNIVERSAL
SPIRITUAL LAWS ~

When one experiences this shift in the inner world, through Awakening and realizing the Divine's true nature, one's sense of perception is aligned with THIS FIELD of Grace, thus working in perfect harmony with the Universal Spiritual Laws of the Universe.

Here are some examples of these Laws:

1.) Law of Action ~ The Law of Action states that we must move in the direction of our desires in order to achieve them. We must engage in some action that supports what we think about and dream about.
2.) Law of Attraction ~ The resonance (vibration) of our thoughts, actions, and words all "attract" like vibration. So *"like attracts like"*.
3.) Law of Oneness ~ There is ONE consciousness that pervades ALL life ~ this is God Consciousness, thus interconnecting *ALL LIFE* ~

Have you ever wondered why you have tried to utilize one of these Laws, but to no avail? It is because Grace is necessary to fuel these Laws into motion ~ So in essence, mankind's limited perception right now is such that Grace is the missing link from our lives, with this limited perception only fueling the ego; mankind is thus cut off from successfully utilizing the Spiritual Laws of the Universe.

What needs to happen, and IS happening right NOW:

THE AWAKENING OF MANKIND THROUGH INDIVIDUALS LIKE YOU ~

The sense of "self" dissolves, and all that is left is the perception of Divine consciousness, "inter"-acting in perfect harmony and oneness with THE FIELD of Divine consciousness everywhere.

Deeksha and its role on the planet now:

DEEKSHA ADDS COSMIC ENERGY TO ALL SPIRITUAL TRAINING

THIS = GALACTIC TRAINING

DEEKSHA brings the Spiritual Training as an EXPERIENCE ~

The Spiritual Laws will no longer just be a belief system or concept.

Deeksha, brought to the planet on a mass scale now by the Oneness University in southern India, is available worldwide through specific processes to initiate Awakening ~ This is sweeping across the globe. Tap in and join along; your life will be forever transformed, and you will affect everyone and everything around you to resonate at a higher vibration. Collectively, this is *shifting* the whole planet ~

~ ONE person does make a difference ~

3

LIFE IS THE PROCESS ~

Life is an ongoing process of acceptance of the *"what is"*. Acceptance means "accept"-ing Grace in, which means *a lack of resistance*.

Resistance
= Blocking life
= Blocking Divine Grace ~

"ALLOW"-ing the flow of the Divine Presence in
= at ONE with the Divine Presence
= ONENESS ~

When resistance drops automatically, Divine Grace has access to fill up each and every cell of your being.

4

THE "NATURE" OF THE DIVINE PRESENCE ~

The Divine Presence is a force FIELD, a very living FIELD, which directly "inter"-acts with us ~

The Presence *IS* a *living, breathing* force FIELD that has to be nurtured, praised, and witnessed; all for it to interact with each of us in the human species! If we don't praise it, it will not interact. Sadhana (spiritual practice) is so important. Invoke and praise ~ invoke the Divine Presence, and praise it. Praise THIS FIELD, until there is a constant flow of praise happening automatically. The sadhana of invoking the Presence is our responsibility to keep doing it, until it is naturally there ~ REALIZE THE IMPORTANCE OF SADHANA ~

The Divine Presence will descend into individuals and merge with the person in oneness. This force FIELD is a rushing river of Grace flowing through. It descends as a tsunami of Grace, ripping through the chakras, shattering "the walls" of the mind, breaking open the cement walls of the heart, as a current of pure Universal Energy rushing in and out of every cell of the being ~

There will no longer be a sense of a "controller," or a sense of a "separate I." There is just the realization of a complete VOID, and that "it all IS happening automatically" ~

The nature of the Divine is that it has to be praised. We activate the FIELD of Grace by praising it! Start praising the Divine for insights, wisdoms, and revelations you receive.

Realize the *true nature* of the Divine Presence ~ it must be praised. This is simply in accordance with the Universal Spiritual Laws. Praising it is how it is activated, how it interacts with us.

5

HUMILITY ~

Pure arrogance may rule your life. Is your life ruled by these statements?

* ★ "I can manifest things to happen"
* ★ "I am great at making things happen"

These statements are a falsehood. The Divine is doing EVERYTHING; there is no "I" capable of doing any of this. The whole concept of "me" manifesting is so foolish, this is the opposite of HUMILITY!

Is humility simply an intellectual concept? Realizing humility means there is no "I," it is only pure Presence, the hand of the Divine doing everything ~ The experiential realization of humility is one of the Divine flowing through, with no "controller" doing any great things in one's life. In fact, the greater the deeds one does in life actually means one has more *humility;* it means the greater the hand of Divine Grace in one's life! When one is successful, it is all due to the Divine hand in life.

Is there *arrogance* with your relationship with the Divine? Realize there is no "ruler" over the Divine, there is no "controller" over the Divine, and there is no manifester. How could there be an "I" controlling the Divine? This is illusion. How could the "separate self" do anything at all ~ only Grace can do it all. You can only witness it, praise it, acknowledge it, and allow it ~

You can still do great things for the planet, but have the realization of humility that the Divine Presence is working through you. Humility is such a hard intellectual concept to grasp, especially when living a very abundant lifestyle. But now realize the greater the life one lives, the greater the abundance actually equals the greater the Divine hand in life being responsible for this!

6

YOUR "ROLE" IS TO PRAISE, RECOGNIZE, ALLOW, AND CONVERSE WTH GRACE ~

There are Divine angels everywhere in the form of people, "peering" at you from everywhere; do you not "SEE"? It is exquisite! Everywhere you look, SEE the Divine is actually looking back at you: through strangers, family members, animals, creatures big and small, trees, flowers, and all nature. Do you frown when someone is looking at you? This really equals blocking the Divine Presence coming through them. Now it is the time to realize that these are ALL Divine angels.

THE FIELD of consciousness is so very thick, experiential, interactive, and responsive, for everyone! Commune with it about everything ~ Praise the Presence all day long for absolutely everything! Nothing is too trivial or small to give thanks for.

7

LIFE SHOULD BE AN EXPERIENCE AS FULL ACCEPTANCE, WHICH REALLY EQUALS LACK OF RESISTANCE ~

Resistance equals "blocking out life," which equals **blocking Divine Grace**. When accepting the flow of Divine Presence in, it equals being at "ONE" with Divine Grace, which equals **ONENESS**. This is based on a very simple Universal premise. When resistance dissolves, Divine Grace then has complete access to fill up each and every cell!

In your relationships, is there the illusion (story) that "the other" does not appreciate you or is holding you back? This is only the sense of separate self, craving and begging for love. This equals the complete blockage of Divine Grace. This is really being in resistance to the other. Where there is resistance to the other, there cannot be acceptance.

Grace is bringing abundance to you through your most important of relationships. ONLY Divine Grace pours through the other: in their eyes, words, and actions. There has never been "another"; it has always been Divine Presence. Now SEE it is all pure Grace pouring through the other to make your life amazing; how did you ever not SEE this before?

When in full acceptance of another, it is the experience of simply observing and experiencing the other. It is exquisite! You will find yourself simply experiencing their every word and action, no need to change anything about them for they are all **DIVINE**

BEINGS! Pure Divine intelligence comes through their every action. The experiencing of the Grace coming through in this way is exquisite.

Experiencing another in one of complete acceptance literally means: "accepting the Divine Grace in," accepting ALL Grace in.

Have you been thinking regularly, "Please transform my partner, so that we will have harmony in our relationship, so that we will have a true connection?" Now this is the cosmic joke because the other has to do NOTHING AT ALL; what it takes is a SHIFT IN CONSCIOUSNESS in you, to bring all resistance into all acceptance. To completely accept another individual, without ANY resistance, is yours to be had. This will be an experiential reality ~

8

FEAR OF ABUNDANCE ~

There are energetic blocks to being able to receive money in that may have stemmed from childhood. For example, you may have been conditioned as a small child that too much money makes couples fight. That couples fight over too little money, and they fight over too much money. Your family may have fought over these issues. These fights can cause great conditionings for you in your adult life and equal an energetic block to receiving abundance in.

Some other issues that may have caused you to block out Grace in the form of money is learning as a child that you can have a lot of abundance, but then it can leave you overnight. The situation can be very painful for all involved and causes a lot of fighting, and it causes a lot of families to break up. You may have had a fear to praise money, because you had the fear of losing it the next day.

Another issue is that you may have learned at a young age the conditioning that money changes a person. It can change your family members. For example, that having a lot of money can turn your husband into a jerk. You also learned that the more money you have, the more stress you have, and the more complicated your life is.

All these years you may have had a black hole in you, the feeling that you were not complete, that you were broken and scarred. You had a lifelong fear that goodness and abundance would never come to such a broken person, that only 'good and proper' individuals lead a very abundant life.

Be kind to yourself with these realizations. It was complete survival mode that you put up a cement wall around your heart. It was all you knew how to do. SEE that this cement wall blocked abundance from you. This wall can be shattered forever by sheer Divine Grace. "BE" with the darkness, fully and completely. Grace can come in and heal the blackness in your heart for good, to infuse it with light forever. There is nothing else for you to do except BE OKAY with your darkness of the past: any trauma, any self-hate, any substance abuse, and any depression. Slow down in life ~ Be gentle on yourself.

9

IT'S THE SAME DIVINE GRACE IN "GOOD" ACTIONS AND "BAD" ACTIONS OF OTHERS ~

Who do you have complete resistance to in your life, based on "bad" actions of this person?

Remember, there is no "other," it **is** only pure Divine Grace coming through. Look back through your whole life; see the Divine Grace that was always that person!

You may ask: "How do I accept this person's past actions that upset me?"

It's the same Divine Grace in good and bad actions, the exact same Grace. All you can do is accept ALL Grace in. There is no such thing as blocking one or the other (for example, good or bad). It is either acceptance or resistance. There is no such thing as good or bad, for it is all Divine.

10

THERE IS NO "I" THAT CAN PICK THE CHOICE OF GOOD OR BAD COMING IN ~

This is **pure arrogance** that we have that choice. We can only accept or resist.

ACCEPTING ALL, ACCEPTING EVERYTHING = "ACCEPT"-ING ALL GRACE IN

RESISTING = BLOCKING GRACE OUT ~

This completely stops the flow of the Universe.

This is a Law of the Universe ~

This is the game the "I" plays: "Oh, I have a choice to let the good or bad in." This is a complete illusion and falsehood. It is all Grace anyways, and there is no "I" to make that choice.

11

GOD-REALIZATION ~

There is no difference between you and God. You are in constant communion with the Divine, constantly "inter"-acting with THE FIELD. THE FIELD of infinite possibilities **is** instantly accessible and tangible. THIS FIELD is the same FIELD that is inside of you. This constant communion as experiential realizations, as Divine conversations!

God realization is being at "ONE" with the force FIELD, where there is no difference between a person and god, where it is all "ONE" force FIELD.

This force FIELD, which is inside everyone, which is "the person," is the same force FIELD which is all around ~ THIS FIELD is nudging energy into the FIELD all around for your desires to come into action ~ Realize the importance of praise for this force FIELD.

12

THE PRAISE ENLIVENS THE FIELD, BRINGS IT TO LIFE ~

PRAISE = ACTIVATING THE VIBRATION OF THE FIELD ~

The vibration in THE FIELD is the same vibration as praise, so by speaking praise, you are speaking the same language as the force FIELD.

~ ONE MUST ACTIVATE THE FORCE FIELD THROUGH PRAISE ~

Praise is very different from gratitude. Praise is the sadhana of simply expressing thanks. It is the act of acknowledging and giving "thanks" for Grace, verbally, either internally or externally. This activates THE FIELD. Praise also activates THE FIELD of gratitude.

PRAISE ACTIVATES THE FIELD ~

PRAISE ALSO ACTIVATES GRATITUDE ~

Gratitude also activates THE FIELD, so praise can be seen as step 1. So it's all about activating THE FIELD, right? That's the goal! Once the shifts of Awakening and God-Realization happen, praise becomes a natural and effortless activity. Until that point, however, one must do the sadhana of praise.

13

PASSION ~

Passion is simply Divine Grace streaming in. There is no passion when there is an "I" or "controller"; how could there be? The "I" blocks Divine Grace, thus blocks passion.

PURE PASSION = PURE DIVINE GRACE STREAMING IN~

How can it be any other way?

There is no "I" to have passion.

PASSION IS DIVINE GRACE ~

The Divine Grace of passion that is "you" ignites the Divine Grace and passion in others.

14

LIFE IS RELATIONSHIP ~

THE GREAT MEANING OF LIFE IS TO *EXPERIENCE ALL LIFE* ~

NO SUCH THING AS PICKING AND CHOOSING ~

PICKING ONLY THE "GOOD EXPERIENCES" = ARROGANCE

Relationships will become so much easier when people wake up = no self. When the self dissolves, then only pure Presence remains to "INTER"-ACT with pure Presence. People put too much emphasis on finding the "perfect" partner. No such thing! This illusion actually = blocking out life and Grace. The "I" thinks it has total control to find a partner with only the "good" qualities.

THIS is the greatest illusion of the separate self and creates *suffering* ~

Life is relationship. It is okay to desire an intimate relationship with another. The problem comes when the searcher blocks out all life in the process. Test it now; look at your own relationships. Are you IN relationship with the other, AND WITH LIFE? This is the most obvious way to let Grace in, through relationships ~ Are you "accept"-ing all Grace in, or are you in *resistance* to the other?

In relationships between men and women, for example, the "I" will never find satisfaction from a relationship, from another person. So what is the point of being in a relationship, especially a "sexual relationship"? Sometimes it seems to bring more trouble than it's worth. Basic premise: there is no "I," there is only the Divine from the other. So ALL experiences are Divine, the good and the so-called "bad." Humans are so scared to experience situations which are labeled as "bad," especially in a relationship. They would rather be alone, which equals blocking life. This is not the point of life.

Being in intimate relationships allows you to experience ALL LIFE in one package: the good + the bad + the ugly = ALL Grace. How amazing is that? People go from one relationship to the next ~ the "I" is only seeking the "good" experiences = pure arrogance that the "I" has this choice. Relationships would be much simpler and easier if people "ACCEPT"-ed it ALL in.

Are you trying so hard to make your relationships only about the "good" qualities? Anytime the other's "bad" traits pop up, do you say: "get rid of it!"? This actually is a form of arrogance; the "I" thinking it can pick and choose the other one's traits.

15

YOUR PARTNER IS YOUR GREATEST GURU ~

To not be in relationship = to not be "INTER"-acting with life

What is your partner reflecting back to you right now? Your partner will reflect back to you all of the things that you have not "seen" or accepted within yourself. Which traits do you not like in the other? Really look into this and SEE that these traits are actually yours ~

Now you SEE that every interaction with another person is pure Divine Grace coming in! There is no such thing as being a "recluse" ~ that choice only equals *blocking out all life*.

LIFE IS RELATIONSHIP! Divine Grace is streaming through seven billion people on the planet, all in very different ways. Enjoy the differences. Honor the differences, for this is Divine Presence meeting Divine Presence in all others!

16

SIGNIFICANCE ~

The "I" pursues "self" significance. After the shift of Awakening and there is no longer a sense of "I", then there is no pursuit of a "self" to have significance.

Even the opposite of this, the "shunning" of self-significance is the game of the "I" ~ an ego game. When the "I" says: "Look at me, I don't seek significance," this is really the same thing as self-significance, for it is the "I" or 'controller' explaining a story. The "I" tries to take credit for the Presence, of course, this = arrogance. After Awakening, there is no "I" to be doing anything, only pure Presence!

17

LIFE IS THE PROCESS ~

Every minute of every day IS utilizing this *Divine consciousness*.

Ask the Divine Presence, "Show me the revelation about my relationship with this person, or that event," and it will all be revealed to you instantly, through this Divine consciousness, through experiential realizations.

With each and every Divine signpost, praise the Divine and laugh out loud! SEE the Divine in everyone and everything. Real life now is so much better than any fiction! Why? Because there is complete magic coursing through you and the Universe ~

18

THE RECOGNITION OF THE DIVINE IN EVERYTHING BRINGS STRONGER AND MORE MIRACULOUS EXPERIENCES ~

Your relationship with the Divine is a symbiotic relationship! The Divine relies on you as much as you rely on the Divine. Praising is so important to activate THE FIELD because it is the same vibration as THE FIELD. Praising *IS* speaking the same language as THE FIELD. The best way to "praise" is to say the simple words of "thank you" for absolutely everything that happens to you during the day. This will create a tremendous cycle of miracles to unfold and will deepen your bond with the Divine universal forces dramatically.

How do you give praise even if don't "feel" it? Realize the simple act of praising THE FIELD will activate THE FIELD. Of course, praising WITH FEELING is exponentially more effective, but this will happen over time. What people must start doing NOW is: praising by speaking the simple words of "thank you." This is the very simple sadhana (spiritual practice) that can happen all day long. Once Awakened, this will be a natural progression.

PRAISING = INTERACTING WITH GRACE

19

THERE IS NO FEAR OF DEATH ~

Divine Grace and *only Divine Grace* leads this physical life! This fear of death really = "blocking life". People spend their whole life "fearing death." Do you know how much light is blocked along with that fear? A huge percentage of Grace is blocked due to this fear! This fear actually paralyzes mankind from actually LIVING their lives ~

Test it now; look around. SEE any person walking by you. Don't you see this? They have this fear = *a fear of living*.

FEAR OF DEATH = FEAR OF LIVING

This is an extraordinary paradox! Think about it for a moment ~

ANY FEAR = A FEAR OF LIFE

Why? Because a fear of "bad experiences" really means a person is blocking all life out, thus = *a fear of life*. Think about it for a moment ~

Think about a person you know who has a disease: in general, what is a common characteristic when a person first finds out they have the disease? What do they start doing? They are so scared of death that they actually stop living. Haven't you noticed this? Their whole life now changes. It now becomes all focused on curing "this disease" = *stopping to live life*. Their whole personality changes, this fear of death literally consumes them, test it now ~

FOR EXAMPLE:
The turnaround point in healing from a life-threatening disease is "ACCEPT"-ANCE ~
Acceptance
= Lack of Resistance, *of disease.*

Once in acceptance of this disease, the person then accepts *all Grace in*. The person then starts to accept EVERYTHING in their life.

So how does one make the shift from resistance into acceptance during a healing situation? Of course it takes a shift and this shift can only come from Divine Grace. Only Divine Grace can bring this shift to a person, and fortunately we have the powerful tool of Deeksha to facilitate these shifts. *Then acceptance is no longer a concept, it is an experiential reality* ~

Again, this is one of the greatest illusions that an "I" chooses when to stay alive and when to die ~ Once this is realized, you will have absolutely no fear of death anymore ~ No fear of tragedy, no fear of plane or auto crashes. It will be realized that the Divine is fully in charge.

20

DEPRESSION = RESISTING ALL LIFE ~

The sweeping epidemic of depression on the planet right now is really because the "I" is so overactive in mankind. This means that mankind is in complete survival mode. Look around; whenever there is an upsurge of the "I" in survival mode, the "I" naturally creates **FEAR**. The "I" thrives on fear and gives it a complete sense of self-significance.

FEAR OF DEATH = FEAR OF DEATH TO SELF, OF EGO

THIS SURVIVAL OF "SELF"= SELF-SIGNIFICANCE

So how is depression related to all this? Because depression = psychological suffering. When the "I" is in survival mode, it = physical suffering, which doesn't necessarily mean a physical ailment. However, it does mean a survival mode of safety, health, and wealth.

So the physical sense of the "I" suffering from fear becomes so great, the fear of death becomes so great, that this is now generated into the psychological suffering; why? Because this feeds that "I."

So much energy is now poured into this psychological suffering. An enormous amount of Universal Energy is consumed by the individual to feed the "I" during depression. So, the "activity of depression" feeds the "I" and actually strengthens it when its very survival is being threatened. Of course, the "I" just changes its course, and thus the condition becomes psychological suffering.

21

THE GLOBAL PERSPECTIVE
OF DEPRESSION ~

Test it now ~ look at your own past with depression, look at your depressed friends, look at people on medication, look at the pharmaceutical business; billions of dollars go into medications for depression.

DEPRESSION = BIG GLOBAL BUSINESS

What is being suggested is that "the powers that be" generate fear through media and various global events so that people remain in shock and in "survival mode." This actually creates the psychological suffering known as depression, and this spreads throughout mankind. This scenario completely disempowers the human race! So when an individual goes to a doctor and describes their depression, guess what the doctor prescribes them? The very powerful prescription pill ~

THIS ALL = THE PERFECT SCENARIO FOR DISEMPOWERING HUMANS ~

YES, this is the bigger picture ~

So what starts perhaps as an individual journey with pain from the past can be completely manipulated into intense FEAR and DEPRESSION.

When you look into the eyes of certain people, can you see "fear"? Of course ~ Fear is energy, a darker energy. Not a bad energy, just dark, which = no light. The more fear = the less light shining through. It is very recognizable when you meet people with so much light shining through. These are the people who have "accept"-ed Grace into their life, accepted life in. Of course, just look around and SEE ~

22

ACCEPTING GRACE INTO ONE'S LIFE GENERATES MORE LIGHT ~

"THIS" = A UNIVERSAL LAW

It becomes a very powerful cycle of Grace. When people are on an upswing of allowing Grace (light) into their life, they are riding this energy, literally, in a spiral moving upwards. The initial step of moving from fear into light is very difficult, especially given the man-made dilemmas of the planet at this time. But it is possible, and it is happening right now through Grace. How could it happen any other way? Grace is the only thing with the "power" to break the conditionings of fear from someone. No "I" can do this, only Grace.

People would transform so much faster if they knew this Law of the Universe. Even conceptually knowing about this can help a person move forward from fear into light. Then of course the real transformation comes, and living **without fear** becomes an experiential reality.

One person does make a difference. One person can change the whole world, and this is due to the web of "INTER"-action. One Grace infused person, being at ONE with the "ALL THAT IS", generates so much light, just by "BE"-ing. This person of light is a <u>BEACON</u> and generates a huge radius of light around him and affects everyone and everything in his Presence.

It is extraordinary! This is because the Divine Presence from you is activating the Divine Presence in the "all that is" all around you

~ in people, creatures, environment, even events. Because THIS FIELD is the same FIELD *all around* ~ it is a very *efficient* FIELD, and the way of transferring energy is instantaneous!

Grace through Deeksha comes in and fuels all Universal Laws, and has the capability of breaking up fear, disbelief, and conditionings ~ It is one of the fastest tools on earth. The ancient esoteric practices now made available to the West through the Oneness University processes are dissolving the self and bringing God-Realization to so many people = Grace through people, all around the planet, spreading like wildfire ~

= A GRACE-INFUSED PLANET

= THE GOLDEN AGE ~

23

UNIVERSAL LAW: DISBELIEF CANCELS OUT ALL "INTER"-ACTION WITH THE FIELD ~

How does this work? Because disbelief sends out an actual vibration, a very low vibration that blocks life = blocking Grace = blocking access to THE FIELD. So disbelief in any form is a type of disempowerment.

Grace can transform disbelief INTO BELIEF ~ in an instant!

The energies started to come into the planet during February 2011 = massive amounts of Grace. These energy FIELDS from the cosmos and the sun are blasting our planet and breaking up disbeliefs instantaneously. It will actually be very painful for some people: physically and emotionally. It takes an enormous rush of energy to break up disbelief as a collective. Grace from the cosmos is the only thing with the power to break the grip of fear that has overtaken the planet. Mankind has an extraordinary window of opportunity right now, with the massive amounts of Grace accessible. Use the Grace, accept it, and utilize it! THIS IS EMPOWERMENT ~

BELIEF ACTIVATES THE FIELD INTO ACTION ~

True 100 percent belief activates THE FIELD to bring this belief into reality. Why?

BECAUSE BELIEF IS SPEAKING *THE SAME LANGUAGE* AS THE FIELD ~

It is so important to speak the same language as THE FIELD ~

This can come in the form of PRAISE, BELIEF, LOVE. Bring all these things to THE FIELD and see what happens; test it! Right now, most people's hearts are dry and closed, shut off from the world ~ however, utilize Deeksha, as this Divine energy instantaneously can open people's hearts!

REALIZE:
THE ALL THAT IS = THE FIELD

AND THIS FIELD RESPONDS IMMEDIATLEY TO: BELIEFS AND DISBELIEFS

25

EMPOWERMENT ~

THE QUANTUM PHYSICS FIELD OF THE LAWS OF THE UNIVERSE + UTILYZING THE ENERGETIC TOOL OF DEEKSHA = EXTREME EMPOWERMENT FOR MANKIND

WHY?

BECAUSE DEEKSHA = GRACE

= COMMUNING WITH THE FIELD

THE EXPERIENTIAL GUIDE TO GRACE, TO THE FIELD ~ *THROUGH DEEKSHA*

Deeksha is Divine Consciousness and sets the creative forces of the Universe into motion.

Every minute of every day IS the process now, being at ONE with THE FIELD ~

THIS FIELD "ripples" with every thought, intention, word spoken, and feeling added to it ~

This ripple is energy. There is just Presence flowing out and interacting with the Presence all around. The web of interaction is so very experiential, from the smallest of interactions all the way to the larger global interactions. There is no difference in the significance of interactions, for they all set the Universe in motion; some are just more powerful than others ~

26

VARIOUS PERSONALITIES ARISING AND FALLING ~

Do you SEE your very strong personalities carrying you through your whole life? For example, do you SEE the shy personality? The warrior personality? The courageous personality? Your life is simply made up of all these various personalities arising and falling, propelling you forward in life.

Take a moment to reflect on your various personalities. Do you consider some of them "good"? Do you consider some of them "bad"? For example, do you have extreme resistance to some? Why is that personality so wrong?

So-called personalities cannot be termed as "good or bad." There will be a full acceptance of ALL of your various personalities ~ SEE how all of these various personalities have actually worked together in perfect harmony to bring you to where you are right now ~

This is all so very extraordinary to SEE! Living in a state of ACCEPTANCE concerning the "true nature" of your various personalities and simply observing them as they are arising and falling brings CONGRUENCY.

CONGRUENCY
= YOUR INNER WORLD EQUALS YOUR OUTER WORLD ~

THIS = NO CONFLICT

**Being incongruent, on the other hand, creates a constant
state of conflict within an individual
= The conflict state.**
THIS IS THE OPPOSITE OF ONENESS STATE ~

The personalities just flow through the "physical being" ~
unblocked, with absolutely no resistance to any of them, arising
and falling when needed.

THIS = TRUE FREEDOM, TRUE LIBERATION ~

27

ALL EMOTIONS = ALL GRACE ~

Now look at your emotion ~ Again do you term some emotions as "good" and some as "bad"? Do you resist certain emotions, such as sadness? ALL emotions are meant to be experienced fully for they all = Divine Grace.

WHAT YOU RESIST . . . PERSISTS ~

This IS how the Universe works. Take the emotion of sadness, for example. If it is constantly being resisted, it can turn into a deep depression very easily. Now, imagine if you had been taught as a child to be completely okay with your sadness whenever it came up. Imagine if this was a class taught in the first grade. Well, it would have made life a lot easier! In fact, teach the kids to accept sadness whenever it pops up. This should be taught for ALL emotions.

Emotions aren't the problem. The "I" is the problem because it is interpreting the emotion as "good or bad," thus creating RESISTANCE to the so-called "bad" emotions. So as long as the person still has a sense of "separate self," a sadhana (spiritual practice) can be practiced of "SEE"-ing and "FEEL"-ing the emotion; this can be taught to kids and adults alike.

ALL EMOTIONS = ALL GRACE

HOW CAN IT BE ANY OTHER WAY?

THE EXPERIENTIAL GUIDE TO GRACE ~

GRACE IS ALL AROUND ~

DEEKSHA IS THE "EXPERIENCING OF GRACE" ~

DEEKSHA IS THE ENERGETIC TOOL TO ACTIVATE THE UNIVERSAL SPIRITUAL LAWS ~

SPIRITUAL LAWS ARE THE FOUNDATION,

DEEKSHA IS THE ENERGETIC TOOL TO REALIZE THEM ~

People in the Western world already know about THE FIELD ~ this information has already been shown to the world. The next step is the importance of Grace, a.k.a. Deeksha, to activate the person to become:

ONE WITH THE FIELD

Deeksha and the ancient Oneness processes fuel the engine of "INTER"-acting with THE FIELD.

DEEKSHA AND GRACE = THE _MISSING LINK_ TO "INTER"-ACTING WITH THE FIELD

RECEIVING GRACE THROUGH DEEKSHA
= THE KEYS TO THE KINGDOM

THIS IS TRUE LIBERATION
= AWAKENED EMPOWERMENT

Empowerment means no need for a guru or middleman ~

It means direct access to Grace. Once you have the KEYS, you then have UNLIMITED POTENTIAL ~

You then have UNLIMITED MANIFESTATION ~

The separate self dissolves, there is no "I" to block the Grace anymore, and the constant river of Grace flows through ~

29

THE MISSING LINK IS THE DISSOLUTION OF THE SELF ~

**Then unlimited manifestation potential
IS THE EXPERIENTIAL REALITY ~**

**The dissolution of the sense of self MUST happen
completely to be "INTER"-acting with the field**

THIS EXPERIENCE = AT ONE WITH THE FIELD

Of course ~ When the "I" dissolves, then only Grace exists, and only Grace can activate THE FIELD. Because it is THE EXACT SAME FIELD! So the sense of "I" actually blocks the Grace from "inter"-acting with THE FIELD until the shifts of Awakening and God-Realization happen. Once these shifts occur, then the individual is in perfect harmony with the Laws of the Universe ~ Then the individual is Grace infused and Grace driven.

The missing link is becoming Awakened and God-Realized when relating to THE FIELD. Some information out there at this time might cause confusion, because the books are about manifesting and "secrets" to "attracting" what you want in life. However, these books assume that an "I" is capable of manifesting anything. Only Grace attracts and manifests ~

30

THE LIFE OF THE "I" = BLOCKING LIFE AND GRACE ~

WHICH = NO LIFE AT ALL, NO LIVING, JUST MERELY EXISTING ~

The "I" simply exists and survives. Once Awakened, the "I" dissolves and all that remains is ***"THE LIFE"***.

"THE LIFE" **IS HERE, NOW!**

TO LIVE
= FREEDOM

PURE GRACE FLOWING THROUGH YOU AND GUIDING YOU,
AS YOU ~

31

FORGIVENESS ~

True forgiveness is a "heart process" ~

Until your heart forgives, you are in resistance, especially to the person that "hurt" you. But actually your resistance remains to ALL people and experiences.

There is a residue of this pain in your heart, which actually blocks ALL GRACE COMING IN ~

Forgiveness is NOT a psychological concept ~

It is an experience of the heart, which must be activated by Grace ~

No "I" has the ability to forgive; Grace is the only thing that can forgive anyone. The "I" holds grudges, doesn't forgive, and is very stubborn. This all gives the "I" a sense of self-significance, of survival. Only Grace will unlock the heart. But what really needs to happen is full dissolution of the SELF, for then automatic forgiveness is in the heart to all ~

~YOU ARE LEARNING THE LAWS OF THE UNIVERSE BY EXPERIENCE . . .

IT HAS BEEN UNLOCKED ~

32

UTILYZE THESE REVELATIONS AND UNIVERSAL LAWS ~

Record them, put them into play into your own life, master them ~

When you share the Universal Laws with others, you MASTER them yourself ~

Speak, speak, speak these insights and share them with others.

For this = a huge way of ACTIVATING THE FIELD and is a UNIVERSAL LAW

SPEAKING ABOUT THE DIVINE PRESENCE

= PRAISING THE DIVINE PRESENCE

= ACKNOWLEDGING THE HAND OF THE DIVINE IN LIFE

= ACTIVATING THE FIELD ~

So now don't you SEE how important this all is?

NOW is integration time, to fully integrate god consciousness into your experience ~

For this all = acceleration and deepening with your Divine. Utilize THE FIELD *to process* everything, and for insights and revelations ~

THE FIELD

= THE FRIEND

= ONE BIG "INTER"-ACTIVE AND RESPONSIVE FIELD

= THE MAGIC FIELD

The floodgates of Grace are opened by the Divine Presence, for the flow of god consciousness to stream through, a freight train of cosmic consciousness.

33

THIS IS THE GRACE-FILLED LIFE ~

A GRACE-FILLED LIFE MEANS ACCEPTING ALL
LIFE IN, ALL GRACE IN

A LIFE WITHOUT THE SENSE OF "SELF"

= A GRACE-FILLED LIFE

A LIFE FILLED WITH GRACE

= A LIFE FILLED WITH ABUNDANCE

HOW DOES ONE ACCESS A GRACE-FILLED LIFE?

BY THE SENSE OF "SELF" DISSOLVING ~

UTILIZE DEEKSHA AND ALL OF THE ONENESS
PROCESSES!

AWAKENING AND GOD-REALIZATION IS
ACCESSIBLE TO ALL ~

THE "HOW" IN LIFE

= THE GRACE FLOWING THROUGH YOU

= "INTER"-ACTING WITH THE FIELD TO BRING
ALL THESE EXPERIENCES TO YOU

= THE DIVINE "INTER"-ACTING WITH THE DIVINE ~

Some people accept Grace more than others. Some channel Grace more. It's okay, not right or wrong. One way is not better than the other way. It just means some people channel AMAZING amounts of Grace. Experiment with this; test it. You might be more drawn to spend time with the people who channel the most amount of Grace.

THIS IS THE LIFE ~

TIME TO IMMERSE YOURSELF IN THIS LIFE!

34

THE ENERGETIC LAW OF BELIEF ~

**100 PERCENT BELIEF =
100 PERCENT ACTIVATING THE FIELD ~**

**DISBELIEF = BLOCKING THE FIELD OF "INTER"-
ACTION ~**

35

SHINE YOUR LIGHT, YOU ARE A BEACON OF LIGHT ~

NOW IS <u>YOUR</u> TIME ~

So much fear is being generated by media sources. For example, look at the fear that was generated by the nuclear fallout situation in Japan in 2011 ~ The media churns so much fear about EVERYTHING, so the public has so much fear. Shine your light, live your life, this is showing people the way!

36

THE TIME IS NOW~

The outer shift happening on the planet and the inner shifts happening within mankind are in complete relationship with each other. This is a Universal Law; there cannot be one without the other.

THE OUTER WORLD REFLECTS THE INNER WORLD
= THE CONNECTEDNESS OF ALL LIFE

= THE WEB OF "INTER"-ACTION

If you wish to transform the outer life, transform the inner life. The events are not mutually exclusive; they are in complete "relation" to each other, of course!

SUFFERING = THE PERCEPTION OF EXTERNAL EVENTS ~

For example, the crisis that happened in Japan, the nuclear fallout = OUTER TRANSFORMATION. This triggers inner transformation. Just wait and see; there is a new paradigm of "clean energy" coming out of the nuclear fallout. This must happen to shift the paradigm of energy consumption. Remember: all events and all earth changes = all Grace! How could it ever not be? Now is the time of outer transformation, this Earth shifting, for this will affect all on the globe.

Now you realize the complete necessity of becoming an Awakened being, for this individual is a "BE"-ing walking in Grace, a "BE"-ing walking through fear. This is it. It is a pretty simple concept, it can't be practiced; it just IS. An Awakened being walks in the Avataric Light and "activates" others around him. Remember, only a very small percentage on the globe will become Awakened in the next few years, that is all that is needed to shift the outer ~

37

WE ARE IN THE GREATEST SHIFT OF THE AGES; ACTIVELY PARTICIPATE IN IT ~

THE SHIFT IS AFFECTING ALL ~

PEOPLE *MUST* SHIFT CONSCIOUSNESS

= THE GREATEST WORK TO BE DONE AT THIS TIME ~

PEOPLE *MUST* HELP OTHERS TO SHIFT CONSCIOUSNESS

= THE GREATEST WORK TO BE DONE AT THIS TIME ~

AN AWAKENED BEING

= A STABLE BEING

= COMPLETELY UNAFFECTED BY OUTER SHIFTINGS

= STABILITY OF PLANET

= THE IMPORTANCE OF AWAKENING ~

AWAKENING = EMPOWERMENT

AN AWAKENED BEING

= A "BE"-ING "IN ACTION"

= "INTER"-ACTING WITH LIFE

= LIVING

UNAWAKENED BEING = RESISTING LIFE = BLOCKING LIFE

AN AWAKENED AND GOD-REALIZED BEING

= A SUPER SOLDIER OF LIGHT

A SUPER SOLDIER OF LIGHT

= BEACON OF STABILITY AND COSMIC CONSCIOUSNESS

38

ALL OF YOUR DIVINE GIFTS MUST NOW BE UTILIZED ~

All of your Divine gifts now must be utilized, for this is a way to give thanks to your Divine ~

Divine gifts that are not utilized
= blocking Grace
= blocking a person's purpose on the planet.

"OWN" YOUR GIFTS

= "MASTER" YOUR GIFTS

= MASTER OF THE LIFE.

GIFTS THAT AREN'T UTILIZED WILL DISSIPATE
= UNIVERSAL LAW ~

GIFTS *MUST* BE ACTIVELY UTILIZED FOR THE BENEFIT OF OTHERS.

GIFTS = GRACE

GIFTS = "INTER"-ACTING WITH THE FIELD

SO YOUR ROLE

= "BE"-ING A SUPER SOLDIER OF LIGHT

= "INTER"-ACTING WITH THE FIELD

THIS = THE HIGHEST PURPOSE OF LIFE RIGHT
NOW ~

THIS TIME = YOUR TIME

OF ACCEPTING ALL GRACE IN ~

= FULL ACTIVATION AS A SUPER SOLDIER OF
LIGHT FOR ONENESS CONSCIOUSNESS ~

SADHANA IS SO VERY IMPORTANT,
ESPECIALLY IN THE WESTERN WORLD ~

PEOPLE MUST DO THE SPIRITUAL PRACTICES
OF SADHANA ~

39

PHYSICAL DEATH ~

Realize that we are all Divine Presence flowing through a physical body. No "I" can control, decide, or stop the death of the physical self ~ that is a complete falsehood. Only Grace decides when physical death occurs. So there is no longer a worry of death of physical self; and no worry of death of others, for it all equals Divine Presence flowing.

The Presence flowing in the physical life is the exact same as the Presence flowing after the physical death ~

It is all just a RIVER of consciousness and bliss. No such thing as "my" body ~ only existence, consciousness, bliss. My body is not my body = this is a complete realization. All it takes is a perceptual shift, to now have no attachment or suffering of the physical embodiment. The rushing river of Presence courses through this body, all day long.

40

EARTH CHANGES ~

Earth changes are coming whether we "know" about them or not.

EARTH CHANGES = ALL GRACE COMING IN

THERE IS NOTHING TO DO, CONTROL, OR CHANGE ABOUT THE SITUATION ANYWAYS

= AN AWAKENED REALITY

AWAKENED ONES

= NO "REACTION" TO OUTER SITUATIONS

= RESPONSIVE MODE

= LACK OF RESISTANCE

= DIVINE GRACE FLOWING THROUGH

AWAKENED ONES

=THE "RESPONSIVE" TEAM ON THE PLANET, THE "RESPONSE" TEAM OF STABILTY

IT DOES NOT MATTER WHERE THE AWAKENED ONES ARE LOCATED ON THE PLANET, THEY ALL ACT AS A COLLECTIVE STABILIZING FORCE

= STABILIZING THE FIELD OF THE PLANET

= STABILIZING THE MORPHOGENIC FIELD

= AN ENERGY EXCHANGE

RESPONSIVE MODE NEGATES SO MUCH OF THE REACTIONARY MODE

~ THIS IS A LAW OF THE UNIVERSE ~

ONE RESPONSIVE BEING far outweighs many *"reactionary"* beings. All it takes is one person who is responding to a situation to bring a sense of calm and joy to the whole situation.

It is all up to the sacred contracts anyway, of each individual person alive today, as to what they will be experiencing during *THE GREAT SHIFT.* The best thing to help the public during these Earth Changes is to be an Awakened and God-Realized Being ~ The next best thing is to help facilitate Awakening for people all around you ~

41

THE UNIVERSAL LAWS ARE UNLOCKED BY DEEKSHA ~

BEING ONE WITH THE "ALL THAT IS" IS NOT AN ACHIEVEMENT,
IT IS A *SHIFT* FROM GRACE ~

IT IS BEING *AT ONE* WITH THE UNIVERSAL SPIRITUAL LAWS OF THE UNIVERSE ~

IT IS ONE THING TO JUST RECEIVE GRACE.
IT IS A WHOLE OTHER THING TO FOCUS AND DIRECT IT CONSCIOUSLY, THUS MASTERING GOD CONSCIOUSNESS ~

THIS IS WHY YOU ARE HERE ON THE PLANET AT THIS TIME,
TO BE AT ONE WITH THE ALL THAT IS ~

EMBODYING UNIVERSAL ENERGY IN THE PHYSICAL FORM

= "BE"-ING THE LINK BETWEEN HEAVEN AND EARTH.

= AN ACTIVATED SUPER SOLDIER OF LIGHT.

42

YOU ARE A BEACON OF LIGHT ~

SEE "the you" as the link between heaven and earth, in perfect balance and Oneness, as a stabilizing force on the planet ~

YOU

= A MASSIVE "LIGHT"-HOUSE

The "I" is just an empty vessel, for Grace to flow through. There is the direct link and cycle with the Universal wheel of energy. The better the physical vessel, the better the energy comes through = a Universal Law. The higher vibration of the physical vessel (through diet, yogas, lifestyle, health) the higher vibration is the flow of the ONE that comes through. Taking care of the physical vessel is a karmic wheel of relationship with the body. It is all based on karma; how could it ever not be?

SO LIKE VIBRATION ATTRACTS LIKE VIBRATION, IN ALL AREAS OF YOUR LIFE = LAW OF THE UNIVERSE

43

YOUR LIFE IS THE MIRACLE ~

The more Grace you allow in, the more your life is the miracle! Again it is a Universal Law:

MORE ALLOWANCE + MORE ACCEPTANCE

= THE MORE MIRACULOUS GRACE THROUGH YOU,
AS YOU, "INTER"-ACTING WITH THE FIELD ALL AROUND

Once there is no "I" or "controller" to block Grace, then life can only be a miracle! Why? Before the "I" was blocking **MIRACLES OUT.** Now the floodgates are open ~

YOU "ARE" THE MIRACLE!

A walking "miracle of Grace," "INTER"-acting with THE FIELD.

This all equals extreme humility ~

How can it ever not be so?

The recognition of miracles activates more miracles. Even the smallest of miracles needs to be recognized and praised. This is the cycle of energy ~ the only way to interact with THE FIELD is to recognize Grace flowing to me and through me ~ all "inter"-acting within the web of Oneness.

44

YOU ARE A CHILD OF
THE DIVINE ~

The same energy of Presence in the "you" is the same energy as god ~ For mankind, it is just a simple perceptual shift in the brain that we are separate from god. The switch is so easy and simple, but it can ONLY BE ACTIVATED BY Grace. Once activated by Grace, the switch is "on"; you are at a point of "no return."

The whole point of Deeksha and the Oneness processes is to turn this "switch" on ~

This creates very beautiful "BE"-INGS walking on the earth = Activation of them scattered across the planet ~

~THEY ARE THE LINK BETWEEN HEAVEN
AND EARTH:
THE GOD LINK ~

Of course this is how it MUST happen, the Divine Presence must descend into human beings. This IS the whole point of your lives, to be that link.

45

YOU ARE THE LINK OF LIGHT ~

The Presence streams up and down your body, into the heavens and into the earth.

YOU = A MEGA LIGHT CONNECTING HEAVEN AND EARTH ~

You are simply a complete empty vessel of Grace, with enormous amounts of energy pouring through.

PEOPLE MUST GET LINKED UP NOW ~

God-Realization must happen to a certain group of people, a small percentage of people. Humans MUST make this choice as their intention for it to happen. They must do spiritual practice; they must praise the Divine Presence for everything. Then and only then will Grace come in and turn the "switch" on. It MUST be initiated by humans. Grace is all around; it is so ready to be accessed.

Universal Law states:
THE HUMAN *MUST* INITIATE CONTACT FIRST ~

It cannot happen any other way. We all designed "this game" eons ago so that this would happen this way, right NOW ~

Humans initiate link through intention, praise, sadhanas, belief, prayer—so many ways, in fact. But Grace is the thing that fuels all this. So utilize the Grace filled Deeksha, for it is the energetic tool to activate THE FIELD of Grace into motion.

46

YOU ARE DEAR TO YOU ~

So you see, being the LINK OF GOD, between Heaven and Earth, you shower yourself with Grace; all the gifts of Grace are coming from you. ALL are children of god, there is no exception to this. The difference, however, between people is that some are aligned with Grace, which makes them Grace-filled "BE"-ings = a truly Grace-filled life.

Some, however, aren't. There is no right or wrong with this; some people *are not better* than others. It JUST IS and is the realization process. You recognize THIS LINK WITH Grace in others, yes? It is very easy to spot ~ more and more people will become linked up very soon.

Do you feel tremendous pain sometimes, the pain of others who feel completely separate from the Divine? It is overwhelming, this awareness and Oneness of the others' pain. Some feel so alone, completely forgotten, sad, depressed. Your heart feels all this pain and is completely compassionate at the same time, for these are ALL CHILDREN OF GOD.

You too have felt this same pain in your existence. Now when you feel their pain in your heart, all you can do is ask the Divine for all to get linked up to their god. The ones that don't feel "dear" to their gods feel completely abandoned, orphans, alone in the world to suffer. Have complete empathy right now, and pray they all *REALIZE* their Divine very, very soon.

47

EVERY DAY A NEW AND DYNAMIC FLOW IS BEING ESTABLISHED WITH YOUR DIVINE ~

Grace is reworking absolutely everything about you during these transformative times! Grace is looking after you like the "babies", your gods are descending into you. The Presence is becoming more dynamic, rich, accessible, and responsive every day. THIS IS THE PROCESS; there is no other like it on the planet. There is nothing more important anywhere than full communion with your Divine within THIS FIELD OF GRACE.

YOUR LIFE NOW

= A GRACE-FILLED LIFE

= A GOD-LED LIFE ~

Grace is flowing through the physical vessel; this is why you are here now. You connect to the Divine in infinite ways. You see, you are just an empty vessel now ~ a link to the cosmic frequency of the "one with all that is." Anything you want to access is yours to experience and realize.

48

THE DIVINE IS DEPENDENT ON MANKIND ~

"God is dependent on the devotee," of course! This is the ONLY way it can happen. It goes back to the simple Universal Law: "thought creates reality." Once a human masters this and owns it as their own = completely empowered human being. This is the point of life = to become empowered! The empowered being utilizes this law in all areas of life; for example, being a successful businessman, having good health, and being in a good relationship. So a person must also use this law spiritually; and for Awakening and God-Realization ~ of course!

This is always the case:

~THERE ARE NO EXCEPTIONS TO UNIVERSAL LAWS ~

When you aren't focused on your Divine, then your god won't be focused on you, simple as that ~ One cannot take the intimate bond with the Divine for granted, EVER. The minute you take the Divine for granted = the cancellation of the bond. This is a Universal Law for all things in your life.

The minute you take anybody or anything or any situation for granted, it will leave. Taking things for granted = INGRATITUDE = blocking Grace from coming into your life. The minute you stop praising the Divine = the minute the Divine stops "INTER"-acting with you. This is a very simple Universal principal. All Grace must be praised, and all realizations must be praised.

49

TAKING ANYTHING FOR GRANTED IN LIFE IS ACTUALLY THE ENERGETIC WAY OF ASKING IT TO LEAVE YOUR LIFE ~

PAY ATTENTION TO THE PEOPLE AND THINGS YOU LOVE IN LIFE, HONOR THEM EVERY DAY ~

Your thought creates reality, so whatever you are focusing your attention on, both consciously and unconsciously, will bring these things into your life. Ingratitude is the biggest of all traits of mankind right now.

This is simply due to the switch of that part of the brain being turned off = LACK OF GRATITUDE = LACK OF SACREDNESS FOR ALL LIFE = BLOCKING ALL GRACE.

50

THE SACREDNESS OF ALL
LIFE = ALL GRACE ~

When this switch is turned off = this exact life that mankind has created for himself. For example, a planet filled with poverty, environmental destruction, greed, wars, and so on. With the shifts of Awakening and God-Realization, the shift of sacredness and gratitude is turned ON.

When others release pain, you will feel it too. When they cry, you cry. Because ALL LIFE is sacred, even suffering, you may experience all of this suffering in your heart. The natural by product of this is also feeling so much love and compassion in your heart too.

Experience the pain as the same as bliss running through your body. Your Divine Grace is "inter"-acting and connecting with their Divine Grace, in one big web of Oneness. They are all children of god, your brothers and sisters! This is Oneness, experiencing the pain and suffering of a complete stranger, in every single cell of your being. There is no "I" to judge, no "I" to perceive, no "I" to resist or block; it is only Grace interacting with Grace ~

51

BHAKTAS ARE THE DEVOTEES OF THE DIVINE PRESENCE ~

Being devoted to the Divine means being so in love with the Divine, that all you can do is DEVOTE. Bhaktas only praise and worship the Divine in whichever form works best for them. You see, it's all the same energy. Each form = a different manifestation of the god energy. So Oneness is actively creating Bhaktas, through the "quick-route" of Awakening and God-Realization. How they honor the Divine will be specific to their own nature. There are infinite ways to bond to the Divine.

FIND YOUR OWN WAY TO BE DEVOTIONAL TO THE DIVINE ~

It could be acknowledging the Divine through "words," either written or spoken. Some people will sing songs, some will dance, and so on. Find the most powerful way for you! Experience this right now; the Presence is flowing through the physical vessel, what is your most blissful way to devote?

Bliss = true communion with your god. This takes tremendous focus and dedication, and fuels more of the same to come through you. It is also a perfectly natural and wonderful way to become completely empowered within the Universe, to become completely bonded with your Divine.

Now imagine thousands and thousands of Bhaktas walking the planet, scattered everywhere. They are in complete communion with god in their own special way. These are "THE AWAKENED

ONES TO GOD." They are walking with god, as god. Imagine the Grace pouring through these individuals = creating a web of Grace.

This web of Grace, through all the devotion and karmic acts, activates the entire morphogenic FIELD of the whole planet.

THIS

= THE GOLDEN AGE

= THE AGE OF THE "ACTIVATED SUPER SOLDIERS OF LIGHT" ~

The golden age must be activated by these "awakened ones." It cannot happen any other way. The awakened ones = the human "BE"-ing the link between heaven and earth. This is the descent of the Divine on planet earth.

You have seen that being activated and consciously activating THE FIELD of Grace exponentially increases the flow of god, yes? Of course! When the cosmic energies flow through you in your way, it = a huge vortex of light being created. This is a beacon of light, a lighthouse. This is your way.

So each of the "Bhaktas" will have their own way. Grace IS them, so Grace will shine THROUGH them, with their own gifts.

PLEASE REMEMBER:

ALL GIFTS = ALL GRACE

As with all Grace, all gifts must be praised, especially if it is a "new gift" ~

52

THE ONENESS PHENOMENON ~

= THE DIVINE + THE AWAKENED "ONES"

The Divine is dependent on "THE ONES" to usher in the Golden Age. This was the pact, the allegiance. No one person was going to come and do it all. It never could happen that way. The golden age must come through the GOD-FILLED ONES.

**THE ONENESS PHENOMENON =
THE FULL DESCENT OF THE DIVINE INTO MANKIND ~**

The "ONES" = the Divine Vehicles of the Oneness Phenomenon = the "god link" between heaven and earth, working together toward the common goal of planetary Awakening.
What the planet needs now are the:
ACTIVATED AWAKENED ONES,
THESE SUPER SOLDIERS OF LIGHT ~

53

THE VARIOUS ASPECTS
OF THE GOD BOND ~

The bond that you have with your Divine Presence can take on so many different forms, and is completely dependent on you. For example: is your Divine your teacher where you are the student? Is your Divine your beloved, where you are the lover? Is your Divine your master, with you as the servant?

Bow to your Divine Presence, to the Grace bestowing "ALL THIS" through you. Recognize all the various aspects of this relationship; it is one of continual growth and transformation. The Divine is so dynamic in your life, and realize it will continue to be dynamic in infinite ways.

The experience of God-Realization is a process of utilizing the Universal Laws and Principles. For example, the teaching that "God is dependent on the devotee" can be seen as simply utilizing the *Law of Action*. So this ever dynamic bond with God continues to evolve, morph, and change the more you consciously "build this relationship"; it is fantastic ~

54

MERELY EXISTING CREATES
INSENSITIVITIES TO OTHERS ~

Simply existing creates "insensitivities" to all those around you, does it not? This includes nature + animals = ALL LIFE. The nature of mankind right now, because the collective consciousness is so very low, is that the mere act of existing WILL create insensitivities to others because the parietal lobe (in the brain) is so very active. This = reactionary mode. The majority of the whole planet is in reactionary mode! It is simply a matter of what part of the brain is too active in the collective mind of mankind. So people "simply existing" causes great insensitivities to ALL LIFE all around them. Experience how this realization = helplessness. Then you will see that it is futile to try to be anything other than insensitive ~

People must ask for Grace to come in and give them this quality of "being sensitive." Being Awakened and God-Realized stops this Universal Energy Cycle of "reactionary mode" immediately, once an individual makes this "shift" through Grace. The cycle is stopped, and then all life around this person stops being in reactionary mode too, because of the energetic Law of the Universe. All that's left is the "responsive mode."

55

HUMANS DO NOT HAVE THE CAPACITY TO BE "ALIVE" UNTIL THE SWITCH IS TURNED "ON" ~

Humans do not have the capacity to be alive until the switch is turned "on" and all of the senses are activated completely. Up until that point, it is a life of the "I," which we realize = NO LIFE AT ALL.

GRACE = LIFE

So until the floodgates of Grace have been opened by the shifts of perception, only the "I" exists, unable to connect with anybody or anything. That is the state of mankind right now. But no matter, the floodgates are being opened in so many people around the planet. It is happening very rapidly now.

THE ESSENCE OF WAKING UP =

"THE LIFE" HAS BEEN PERMANENTLY SWITCHED ON ~

The more withdrawn a person is to life all around them (to people, places, things) the more DEAD the person is. Very little growth can happen. This creates a downward spiral, even depression. Only Grace can lift this person up! Grace is the miracle that can make this happen ~

56

ATMAN ~

**ATMAN CONSCIOUSNESS
= THE BIG "I AM"**

= THE ALL THAT IS ~

ATMAN = BEING ONE WITH ALL THAT IS

ANY experience is yours to be had. This = infinite accessibility to the ALL THAT IS. You see, the formless takes form when you name it. By utilizing Atman consciousness, everything opens up to you. Through Atman, you are able to experience any other god that you choose. Just ask for full communion and experience that.

ATMAN

= AT ONE

= ONENESS

**ATMAN
= THE FORMLESS ONE**

**All gods are a piece of this formless ONE, thus =
god in form.
Sri Amma and Sri Bhagavan ARE a piece of Atman
in physical form. So were Jesus, Buddha, and all of the**

great Avatars throughout history. Gods in the physical form are the manifest form of Atman.

ALL GODS AND GODDESSESS
= THE MANIFEST FORM OF ATMAN

ATMAN _IS_ THE ALL THAT IS ~
ATMAN WILL HAVE YOU EXPERIENCE THE
ANSWER
= "THE PROCESS",
AS GOD CONSCIOUSNESS ~

This is all life is, simply a process of realizations. What is different now is you have access to the ONE THAT ALL IS = ATMAN. You SEE and experience the process. Before, you were simply reacting to the process.

57

BEING IN LOVE, AS LOVE ~

Wake up "in love", in love with all life, all pervasive love, drunk on love, your body blissfully feeling love everywhere

= A BEING OF LOVE

= LOVE radiating out of you into the world, love flowing through all your veins, your heart is the organ pumping pure love, your whole chest center alive, awake, radiating pure Oneness light. Swoon with love, with ecstasy, with gratitude, with praise for your beloved, your master, your god!

A BEING IN LOVE = A BEING OF LOVE

NOW YOUR LIFE = BEING "IN LOVE" WITH ALL OTHERS

THE OTHERS BEING SO "ALIVE" IN YOU ~

The billions of cells of your being break open with pure bliss and ecstasy when you are connecting with others. It is insanely exquisite! Even a person's voice will rip through your body in pure ecstasy and oneness. Bliss is the natural birthright from "home." You are experiencing "home" now together with others as BLISS. Enjoy it and soak it up, for life is experiencing the body in all ways: BLISS, LOVE, and JOY.

BEING VERY ALIVE AND BEING ALIVE IN RELATION TO OTHERS ~

MERE EXISTENCE = EXQUISITE BLISS!

Awakening and God–Realization = "this" existence, one of complete bliss and joy. Why? Because there is absolutely no resistance to anyone or anything. There is only full acceptance = a life of Grace.

This is what the human body is designed for = a very blissful experience filled with feeling in the body. Even pain, anger, jealousy: all transmute into bliss, of course! Even pain turns into exquisite bliss!

58

LOVE IS MOTION ~

A "being" in love

= A "being" IN motion

= An "activated" being

= A humble "serve"-ant of the planet ~

To serve IS to love ~

To love IS to serve ~

To be "in love" with ALL life

= The greatest gift of Grace to the planet ~

Love permeates every cell in ecstasy. Love is the absence of fear. Love now has access to every single cell, tissue, and fiber of your being. This is your natural birthright, the birthright for ALL! How could it ever not be? Our physical bodies are designed to be in love, to feel all things. Pain, fear, and anger all transmute into sheer physical bliss, exquisitely.

ALL THIS

= an exquisite existence

= a paradise in and out and all around

= "a paradise found"

after being lost for so long in the torture of self and suffering ~

Now just "BEING" is exquisite ~ BE the lover, the lover of ALL life, in and out and all around. Swoon with love, in a Grace-filled physical vessel.

Swoon now + swoon always

= your existence

= your birthright which must be honored and praised all day, every day!

59

LIVING A LIFE FREE OF FEAR ~

You see: all fears = blocking all Grace = blocking vital life force = stopping the flow of life dead in its track. Fear completely immobilizes a person; the body is thrown in complete resistance to the "what is", all the body's cells frozen in anticipation of "What if this happens?" You have already "realized" that resistance does not equal oneness.

FEAR = COMPLETE REACTIVE MODE

Fears = thought-forms = mental constructs of a "supposed" outcome.

Very simple premise of "thought creating reality."

Mankind is operating off its collective "fears" right now, which boils down to "fear of survival." Fears block Grace coming into a person's life; how can it be any other way?

Fear

= paralysis of life

= no way to live at all ~

~ NOT equal to *LIVING* ~

When a person is free of most of his life's fears, the body is no longer in resistance and is now in acceptance. Awakening and

God-Realization smashes fears apart in a second; you "wake up" free of most fears. This process = "accept"-ing all Grace in. This equals true freedom and liberation. What is left is Grace, and only Grace resides in the physical vessel. Grace in the form of love, rapture, pure bliss, and joy now pervade the body. These rise as the kundalini throttle is full "on". Use your own experience right now. Are you experiencing pure heavenly bliss in your body and the feeling of "being in love" with all life? This = a very beautiful existence.

~ THIS IS HEAVEN ON EARTH ~

You see, fear is one of the most powerful thought-forms on the planet right now, one that is so easily manipulated by the "powers that be" through media, control mechanisms, and so on. Imagine the whole planet gripped in fear = the REALITY today.

Mankind cannot do anything about its fears, just be conscious of them. Grace and only Grace can break up these mental constructs. Mankind must surrender to Grace. SEE this process happening right now for all of mankind, fear instantly being replaced by LOVE ~

60

ABSENCE OF FEAR = LOVE ~

Love is actually all around, just like Grace. There is a *field of love* waiting to be accessed.

LOVE = GRACE

Now imagine a planet FREE of the grip of fear =

~ THE GOLDEN AGE ~

Imagine all humans "BE"-ING in love. This shift is starting to happen and is growing exponentially these coming years. Being "in love" is contagious.

One Awakened and God-Realized being = a "BE"-ING in love = a being "of" love. Love then radiates out and affects your whole community and sphere of influence. Just watch and see for yourself. This happens without effort, it is the natural state of this "love being", "inter"-acting with THE FIELD of Grace. It's the Universal law: "like attracts like."

So Oneness is sending Awakened and God-Realized beings out into the world, covering the whole planet = the greatest work of mankind right now! Thus is the importance of the work that Oneness is doing right now all across the planet ~

61

OPPORTUNITIES ABOUND TO LEARN AND GROW, CONTINUOUSLY ~

You are the student. Having access to ALL consciousness = being in the flow of the Universe. The very nature of the Universe is growth and change, one of constant and unstoppable movement. Once man can get linked to god consciousness, the awareness is then there that even god consciousness is constantly changing, growing, and evolving.

Actively utilizing god consciousness to grow, realize, morph, evolve, and learn = true life mastery = the purpose of life. There is no other purpose but this. Realization IS learning and = the fuel for evolution and growth in consciousness.

Stagnation of growing actually = death = the "state" of mankind now. Because mankind is feeling so separate from god consciousness, how can man learn? That's why mankind keeps making the same mistakes without learning the lessons. It's like bumping around a darkened room your whole life without your arms and legs. Grace is necessary. Grace = the "light" and limbs to master life. Grace is the ONLY light to illuminate this darkened room, to illuminate life.

62

ILLUMINATION = BEING ALIVE ~

Everything is accessible right now, test it, and look around at nature. Ask nature for the lessons and realizations.

Utilize god consciousness to give you lessons from the nature that was surrounding you.

Examples of nature and the surrounding life bringing exquisite lessons:

1.) THE ANTS ~

Ants are the complete representation of TEAMWORK, the web of Oneness to get anything achieved with unity and efficiency, working in relation with others. No such thing as "solo" work. That concept = a falsehood. One ant is completely dependent on all the others to get the job done. There are times to be the "lead" ant and times to be the "serve" ant. The true nature of the ant = teamwork.

2.) FLOWERS IN THE DRY GROUND ~

The flowers in the dry ground represent unwavering faith. There they sit every minute of every day, anticipating without a doubt that rain and sun will fall on them to sustain them. They don't move to another spot, they remain in the same spot, their whole life, in glorious faith that the Divine will deliver everything necessary for them. Their true nature = unwavering FAITH that all will be delivered at the right time.

3.) THE CONSTRUCTION ROCKS ~

The construction rocks are just placed there haphazardly, strewn all over the ground. Yet each rock "knows" its glorious and solid nature and is waiting patiently to be used as a piece of strength. The rock has no need to shout, "Look at me, look at my strength" ~ it just knows and waits patiently to be used by the Divine to place it perfectly in Divine order. True nature of the rocks = patience + strength.

4.) THE DOG JOYFULLY CHASING THE BUTTERFLY ~

This is a seemingly fruitless endeavor, a dog chasing a butterfly; the dog will never catch it. Yet, the dog chases in happy and joyful anticipation. This dance of life reminds us that even fruitless pursuits in life are very joyful, the dance of life being more important than the end result. (See number 5 for the paradox to this.)

5.) LADIES FIXING THE SPRINKLER ~

The ladies beautifully dressed and dry in Indian silk saris, rushing in to fix the sprinklers on the lawn, without hesitation, and getting soaked and muddy. This reminds us that sometimes the end result is more important than the personal desire and comfort. The true nature of these ladies was revealed: that there should be absolutely no hesitation in the pursuit of the higher goal of good and god.

63

UNIVERSAL LAWS ARE TO BE
UTILIZED BY HUMANS ~

This is the point of life. Humans are born with the full purpose to "inter"-act with THE FIELD. It is our birthright, in fact. Right now, humans have forgotten their birthright. This must be REMEMBERED now ~

Right now humans are dead = zombies = not utilizing the gifts of the Universe = a very tragic existence. This is how dis-attached mankind is from ALL life and Grace. Mankind MUST be inspired to utilize the Laws of the Universe. Inspiration MUST happen so people literally tap into the FIELD OF GRACE.

Look: the Universe abounds with gifts! Start recognizing and utilizing these gifts for a true mastery of life, in all areas of life: health, wealth, spirit. The most important is utilizing the Laws in Awakening and God-Realization; then and only then can Grace come in and take care of it.

The "missing link" is the connection to Grace, which is so easily accessed through Deeksha and the Oneness processes. There is top importance of Awakening and God-Realization for individuals spread across the planet. Clarity must be given to a very confused mankind. Oneness is all about stressing the importance of Awakening and God-Realization = educating people on the importance of this. Otherwise, how would people know?

The purpose of being human

= "inter"-acting with ALL around

= ALL GRACE

= THE FIELD ~

This is what the human body is designed for = *BEING AWAKE.* The time is NOW for waking up; you must give them the "wake"-up call, through your words, written and spoken. This is the Avatar's work; the importance must be stressed and shown to the Western people.

64

THIS IS OUR BIRTHRIGHT ~

TO BE A GRACE-FILLED BEING ~

Universal Laws must be recognized and utilized!
Otherwise, what is the point of life?

A human completely disconnected from the Divine +
the Universe

= a blind, deaf, mute orphan

= left to suffer on its own in the garbage of life

= a truly miserable existence.

The emphasis in life has to be on Grace and the
Presence.

This Presence is now readily available to descend into
mankind

= God-Realization

= full liberation and freedom

= a completely empowered and activated human
BEING

This IS our birthright ~

65

SACREDNESS: THE ONE "BEING" PERVADING ALL LIFE ~

The dance of life IS all around. This IS the Oneness Energy, the god consciousness pervading absolutely everything. This is Universal energy. All animate + supposedly inanimate objects pervade with god consciousness = a river of Universal Grace flowing through. Mankind is the only species on the planet with a sense of "separate" self, which completely cuts off the recognition of Oneness. All other species flow in and within Oneness as their true nature. Global coherence among mankind will happen naturally as more of mankind Awaken and become realized to god consciousness. This is the only way for global coherence to happen, which is a very beautiful existence indeed.

For example, take a group of birds flying in perfect Grace and formation: this = perfect Oneness and coherence.

Now just imagine the human species living in such harmony

= a beautiful dance of life

= THE GOLDEN AGE ~

Right now the sense of "separate" self is so great in mankind; humans have "blinders" on and constantly bump into one another and hurt each other without the recognition that all is a perfect dance of life. But this is starting to shift, and the shift will grow exponentially these coming years. Once awakened and realizing god consciousness, the "blinders" are blown off the human existence, and all that remains is a perfect sense of order of Universal energy flowing in and out and all around, interacting with the Presence of ALL life.

66

HEAVEN ON EARTH ~

The Divine is the beloved, you "being" the lover. Your body **IS** love, every cell **ALIVE** with Grace and receptive to ALL life around you. The physical sensation of bliss is ALL PERVASIVE. The heartbeat is pounding in a sea of bliss.

**THIS BEING
= IN LOVE WITH ALL PEOPLE AND ALL LIFE
= "ACCEPT"-ING ALL GRACE IN.**

THIS EXQUISITE EXISTENCE = HEAVEN ON EARTH.

**THE HUMAN "BE"-ING THE LINK BETWEEN
HEAVEN AND EARTH**

= THE GOD LINK ~

**THE PHYSICAL VESSEL IS GOD, WALKING THE
PLANET AS GOD ~**

IN LOVE AND AS LOVE ~

IN BLISS AND AS BLISS ~

IN AVATARIC LIGHT AND AS AVATARIC LIGHT ~

**IN GOD CONSCIOUSNESS AND AS GOD
CONSCIOUSNESS ~**

IN JOY AND AS JOY ~

ENJOYING ALL LIFE, SITUATIONS, PLACES, AND PEOPLE ~

THE SACREDNESS PERVADES ALL LIFE AROUND WITH GOD CONSCIOUSNESS ~

EVERY INTERACTION = THE DANCE OF LIFE ~

THIS IS THE BEAUTIFUL DANCE OF ENERGY AT PLAY WITH LIFE, AND BETWEEN ALL LIFE ~

THERE IS NO RESISTANCE, ONLY ACCEPTANCE

= ONENESS ~

The dance IS god = god consciousness "inter"-acting in all experiences: the insects, the flowers, the trees, and the Universal teachings. God consciousness is in every cell of the body, bustling with energy = "the" energy of the Universe = pure light. The simplistic perfection in all life, surroundings, situations = all life bustling with god consciousness.

God IS perfection, god = perfection.

There is no such thing as imperfection, only the sense of "separate" self has this unique ability to criticize and judge anything as "imperfect," the "I" blocking god consciousness. Once the sense of "I" dissolves into pure Divinity all that remains is god = the recognition is ONE of pure Grace "inter"-acting with pure Grace all around.

67

A BODY OF BLISS ~

People are very "alive" in the physical you, in every single cell of your being. Certain people, just by being in their physical Presence or looking in their eyes, the body experiences pure bliss coursing through your body, experiencing their love as "your" love flowing through your veins.

Just giggle because it is insanely exquisite. Realize the true purpose of "relation"-ships = the other being alive in the physical "you," the billions of cells communicating in perfect Oneness and sacredness.

Every cell in the body has been activated, to receive "Grace" in
= A BODY OF PURE BLISS ~

Every noise, especially loud ones are felt in the body as bliss, no resistance. Every bump on the road of life = activating bliss. The stories that are told by others of their pain and fear, the body feels the various pains and fears spoken about, then transmutes into bliss throughout. Your body is now ALIVE and functioning with all the senses and cells activated!

Every cell is filled with god consciousness, radiating with pure existence, consciousness, bliss ~ all connected in the exquisite FIELD of Grace, the ocean of consciousness within. The body moves on its own accord, billions and billions of cells filled with god consciousness working in perfect coherence, thus = a rushing river of Grace, propelling the body in movement.

The "separate self" has never been "in control" of the body; that is one of the greatest illusions! THIS FIELD of Grace in = the same FIELD of Grace out + all around. The mere act of praising, by the Divine to the Divine = the bond = the same thing = bonded as the exact same vibration in perfect Oneness = bonded to the whole ocean of consciousness that exists.

Thought, intention, prayers, bliss, joy

= all the Divine activating the bigger ocean of DIVINITY~

68

LIFE IS CONSTANT MOTION ~

Every intention, thought, question, act of praise = the Divine itself. Praising = "the" true nature = constant motion. Praising = the acknowledgment of the Divine in every thing, person, and situation. Praising = the language of the Divine = "inter"-acting with THE FIELD of Grace. The Divine has no choice but to respond to praise. Of course, this = Universal law! This law = the exchange of energy: give and take, offer and receive.

Praise + the response of the Divine = "the" bond, the "only" bond that is ever needed in life! The natural flow of the "energy" of praise grows the bond exponentially, which turns into the "discovery" of the Divine. The bond + the discovery morph, evolve, and grow in a constant process of learning, a never-ending process. The gifts of the Divine are infinite!

Discovery = the magical world where the Divine is instantly responsive, attentive, tangible, and very humorous ~

For "this" IS magic = THE magic. To "wake up" to a magic-filled life! God consciousness = the key to this magical world, the "giver" of the magic. All cells connected in Oneness + magic. No sense of "I" could ever be magical, just an illusion. The sense of "I" must get dissolved for the magic to be accessible. The sense of "I" blocks Grace + magic, that is the separate self's sense of "duty" = which gives it existence, of course! Because Grace and magic shatter the "I."

Everything in the Universe utilizes **THE FIELD** constantly and consistently = the forward motion of life. Mankind as a whole is the only species that is not "consciously" utilizing THIS FIELD = a very tragic existence. ALL other life actively participates with **THIS FIELD**; there is no other way to exist.

Man **MUST** "remember" how to utilize **THE FIELD** in a proper way. You see, right now, mankind is utilizing the Laws of the Universe, but in a seriously unconscious and detrimental way! No species can ever escape the Laws. The Laws affect all life. The easiest way for mankind to access and utilize these Laws in a proper way is to realize the Divine, which = your true nature = the magical life.

69

MANY DIVINE "FORMS"
OF THE ALL THAT IS ~

You see, the ALL THAT IS must come in a "form" to a person. This is very critical. The formless must take form; otherwise, it remains just that, formless.

"Forms" are living beings = energy forms = thought-forms = very, very positive thought-forms. The "forms" of Jesus, Buddha, the Hindu gods, Sri Amma and Sri Bhagavan = thoughts-forms which are readily accessible to commune with.

This "form" is the thought-form, while the consciousness associated with the thought-form = pure consciousness. These are pure aspects of Atman = existence, consciousness, bliss.

The thought-forms of Sri Amma and Sri Bhagavan are fueled by Avataric Light and Oneness Consciousness. When this form is your reality in your being, the forms reside there as Avataric Light and Consciousness, accessible instantly. This all occurs in perfect communion with the aspects of Atman.

70

EXISTENCE, CONSCIOUSNESS, BLISS ~

God Consciousness is our true Nature. To be at ONE WITH GOD means there is no sense of "I" or "separate self." Only god consciousness radiates out from your every cell, as existence, consciousness, bliss, thus equaling no separation from god = AS GOD.

Realizing the consciousness of Jesus, Mother Mary, Buddha, the Hindu gods, Sri Amma, and Sri Bhagavan:

IS OUR TRUE NATURE, OUR BIRTHRIGHT ~

Mankind has remained so severely separate from god consciousness for far too long, thus is the reason for the "problems" in the outer world.

THIS SHIFT NOW

= THE SHIFT FROM SEPARATENESS INTO ONENESS ~

71

EYE DEEKSHA = PURE AVATARIC CONSCIOUSNESS ~

Every day you are accessing and discovering AMAZING qualities of your god, for everyday life IS this deepening = massive discovery in a very big way! So much Grace is coming in. Of course this is your experience! Eye Deeksha = pure Avataric Consciousness being transferred to you, in massive amounts ~ Revelations and insights from your Divine will pour in.

Eye Deeksha = a clear shot of experiential revelations, because there is absolutely nothing to get in the way of this Avataric Consciousness. So much is being "activated" by the eye Deeksha ~ so much learning, growing, morphing, and evolving!

THIS IS THE ONENESS PHENOMENON IN ALL ITS GLORY ~

This is Avataric Consciousness being transferred in the most pure + highest quality way possible!

This is filling up the physical body as a true **LIGHTHOUSE OF AVATARIC LIGHT.**

72

NATURE IS VERY MUCH ALIVE
IN THE CELLS OF YOUR BEING ~

The monkeys playing in the trees; the mangoes falling; the birds, the insects, and the flowers ~ Walking along the sacred ground, the rocks, crystals, and quartz are alive in the "you"! The physical "becomes" these properties, of the rocks, of the crystals, of the animals. The magical properties of the crystals are "the you" = crystalline nature. So much energy is radiating from the ground into "the you." The inner silence is so very deep and impenetrable, every outside noise catapults through the body as an explosion.

The smells + the vivid colors = "the you." Did you have any idea that a person could experientially realize what the color "green" is, or "magenta," or "yellow"? Yes, you will experience these very vivid colors as if they were your "true nature". The color green is so intense and all pervasive; it permeates every cell.

The water of the river is "liquid magic" running through and as "the you." The body + senses = so exquisitely ALIVE in perfect communion with any sacred forest. Watch the ants playing and frolicking with each other, experience what the ants are experiencing. Your Divine is giving you this "this reality", this reality of ALIVENESS, there is no other like it! It is the cosmic dance of life, the Grace in this physical body "inter"-acting with the Grace all around, every experience outside = the experience inside.

The Divine really is bestowing ALL the gifts of the cosmos to all of us as the human species, right NOW ~ gifts from ALL dimensions! It no longer is just an intellectual concept and a *hoping*. Even the physical body is being shifted right now, and it does indeed need to be in a certain way to become Awakened and God-Realized. The vibration of this shift is so very high that the body definitely needs a "preparation" period to be able to receive and carry such a high frequency. So there are indeed "steps" to be receiving the highest frequency possible.

73

THE DNA IS BEING SHIFTED FOR AWAKENING ~

Yes, the human body needs to go through very specific processes and adjustments to be able to receive Awakening and God-Realization, for the Avataric light to be "anchored" into the body. So many adjustments must be made. That's the job of the Avatar and the Oneness processes, to align all the koshas (energetic bodies) with the very high vibrations of Awakening and God-Realization.

Awakening and God-Realization

= A dimensional shift

= Accessing the higher realms

= Very high frequencies.

The actual DNA of the individual is being adjusted ~

This = no small undertaking!

It actually = the whole entire Universe conspiring in perfect alignment for this shift to happen to the individual to become:

~ AN ACTIVATED SUPER SOLDIER OF LIGHT ~

To become this super soldier of light, it does take destiny and karma, and also human will. The Divine will absolutely conspire to make all this happen in a cosmic explosion for the individual. The human, however, also needs to put in maximum effort too = a symbiotic relationship. The devotee must reach out to god = a Universal law. It cannot happen any other way. There is a natural progression to the importance placed on Awakening and God-Realization.

Once the "self" dissolves, the individual moves through various stages of ONENESS, until reaching the stage of being "ONE WITH GOD AND THE ALL THAT IS" ~

This then means the "cosmic channels" have been permanently opened, no turning back! Once these cosmic channels have been opened, cosmic downloads start to happen to the DNA, brain, and all the energy bodies. This is an ongoing process, the individual transforming more and more into a "cosmic being".

74

THE "BIRTHING" OF
THE GOLDEN AGE ~

Because of the low state of consciousness of mankind, children now are being born as "children of separation." They carry this "conditioning" and "life program" through their whole life. For some, this conditioning of separation is so extreme, it is termed as "existential suffering," meaning you suffer simply because you exist.

What the planet needs now are "Children of Oneness" being born. How does this happen? The mother needs to be in Oneness and at ONE WITH GOD. Then the birth = a very ecstatic experience.

A long time ago, the birth experience = ONENESS = pure bliss for mom and baby. It was a whole tribal celebration with music, ritual, and chanting.

Children of Oneness being born

= The mother in complete communion with god, baby, cosmos, nature, and community

= The baby being in the experience of ONENESS during the whole birth process ~

The birth tunnel would not be dark, black, and frightening ~

**It would be filled with the high frequency of Avataric
and Cosmic Light and Oneness Consciousness ~**

**Now just imagine all the babies being born on the planet
in this way now:**

= THE GOLDEN AGE INDEED!

Seems impossible, but THIS SHIFT is indeed bringing this
birthing experience back into humanity's reality. This is how it
once was on the planet ~ this reality IS coming back!

75

DEVOTION ~

Dancing and singing in praise to the Divine Presence, this glorious FIELD of Grace ~ "DEVOTION" to the Divine ~ The quickest path to god IS devotion, why? Because devotion activates the field of Grace into motion. Devotion is the energetic "key" to "unlock" the mysteries of the Universe, and to be able to utilize the Universal spiritual laws = the tools given to mankind to be fully empowered.

Devotion in nature is everywhere. This devotion is in dance and praise, of all the critters and creatures. All to the glory of the Divine creation.

The two puppies in glorious frisky play with each other, showing me there are no boundaries needed, fangs bared, paws scratching, the two are so gloriously at peace with each other during this play, no resistance whatsoever, just the exchange of energy ~

The birds singing, all in thanks and praise to the setting sun, the giver of all life and consciousness. How could this beautiful deity not be praised all day long?

The plants, the trees, the critters, all standing up in full glory of praise for this deity, the giver of all life.

Devotion IS a state of Grace, a way of "be"-ing, of interacting with the infinite field of Grace all around.

TO DEVOTE = TO PUT ENERGY INTO MOTION

~ DEVOTION *IS* ENERGY ~

It is energy of pure love, of pure offering, of pure surrendering, to the one, to the supreme being. There is absolutely no-thing to do except devote. The mere act of devotion = surrendering fully to the Grace of the Divine.

76

THE TRUE NATURE OF THE DIVINE IS COINCIDENCES ~

What you term as "chance", as "coincidence", are all simply the synchronicities of the Divine web of Oneness. The Divine connects every one and every thing in one huge web of interconnected happenings. The very nature of this web is harmony, balance, and flow, all working within the Universal Spiritual Laws. It is simply man's "perception" of separation, which limits this bird's eye view. This is man's condition right now. You could say that the state of consciousness is such that man feels so disconnected, thus creating lost, confused, sad, and very lonely humans.

The pain body of mankind right now is so very big, that most everyone is walking around in pain = A LIFE OF PAIN. What is needed is this shift of the Divine where the Divine descends fully into mankind. Then and only then will an individual "see" coincidences, perfectly aligned all day long, automatically happening in perfect orchestration. Coincidences are really the Divine's hand in absolutely everything. When man realizes "the Divine hand in life" = the Golden Age.

77

2012—THE GOLDEN AGE ~

The Golden Age is upon us here and now, in this year of 2012.
This time is the BIRTH of the Golden Age ~

SO NOW, 2012: THE GOLDEN AGE BEGINS ~

God is descending into mankind again, to complete the cycle of
oneness consciousness turning into separation consciousness, and
then turning into oneness consciousness again.

Here you are now, witnessing and actively participating in this
shift! This is no chance encounter ~ This is no chance experience,
these are no chance relationships in the physical realm.

Now, don't you "see" the importance of all this?

78

AWAKENING TO THE DIVINE ~

THE GOLDEN AGE IS SUCH A GLORIOUS TIME FOR MANKIND FOR IT

= THE GREAT *AWAKENING* OF MAN ~

Awakening to what? Awakening to the Divine, of course~

God-Realization IS realizing one is god, one is the Divine, and all that has ever existed is the Divine. No "person" has ever existed in fact. The sense of separate self will be dissolved, thus this illusion that we are separate will vanish from mankind. That's when we say man is LIVING IN THE GOLDEN AGE. Living in Oneness with the Divine.

79

LAW OF DIVINE TIMING ~

The Universe is based on principles. These are known as Universal Principles, or Universal Laws. Everything lives according to these laws.

Synchronicities are the LAW OF DIVINE TIMING, which states: everything WILL happen at the exact right time that it is supposed to happen.

DIVINE TIMING = RIGHT PLACE + RIGHT TIME

What is missing in mankind is simply the perception that this is so. All that is needed is a simple perceptual shift in the brain for man to realize the Divine hand and Divine timing in everything in one's life. Of course, only Grace can bring this shift of Awakening and God-Realization, where the individual then SEES everything HAS ALWAYS been happening at exactly the right time ~ This will only be an intellectual concept until it is experienced.

Then it = an experiential realization and the person will be "shifted".

80

MAXIMUM EXTERNAL EFFORT
IS ALWAYS REQUIRED ~

Synchronicity is simply the Divine moving all the chess pieces on the board game of life. It is so very easy to SEE and experience once the shift happens. Then life = a life of ease. It becomes an effortless flow within Universal forces. Of course, maximum external effort is always required to bring success in any area of life, whether it is health, wealth, relationships, and spiritual awakening.

This **IS** required on the part of man, this **IS** the contract man signed up for when taking incarnation as a human. This is to put in the maximum external effort for the Divine to flow through at maximum potential. Of course, not everyone puts in this maximum external effort, and that is okay. The ONES, however, who continually put in the maximum external effort are the "GREAT ONES". They are the ONES who make the maximum impact on humanity too, in whatever area of specialty is theirs.

You can see it as a ratio: the ONES, who continually put in maximum external effort to create and help the planet, will ultimately bring the maximum amount of benefit to mankind.

Look around. Look around now. Who are the "GREAT ONES"? They are very easy to spot, they are the ONES who never stop growing, never stop expanding, and never stop creating. How can this be so? Because they are in such a state of consciousness where their consciousness is constantly expanding.

Not everyone will be a "GREAT ONE" of course, however, will you be ONE?

81

EXPANSION AND CONTRACTION OF CONSCIOUSNESS ~

**EXPANSION
= GROWTH
= LIVING A LIFE IN FORWARD MOTION ~**

**CONTRACTION
= MOVING BACKWARDS,
WHICH ULTIMATELY LEADS TO NON-
EXISTANCE, DEATH ~**

Everything in your life is either expanding or contracting. You can see it in:

1.) RELATIONSHIPS:

The relationships expanding are filled with LIFE, newness, discovery, growth, and are destined for success.

The relationships that are contracting = bringing death to the relationship = lifeless = doomed for failure.

2.) YOUR HEALTH:

Good health = a body in balance, which also = a body in the expansion phase, where all the bodily functions are thriving and new healthy cells are being created.

Ill health= a body contracting, cells are dying, and bodily functions start to fail.

3.) <u>BUSINESS AND ECONOMICS:</u>

Of course, this is easy to SEE, yes?

Success and making money = EXPANSION

Failure and losing money = CONTRACTION

4.) <u>SPIRITUAL AWAKENING:</u>

A person on the awakening journey, where the kundalini is rising and breaking up emotional charges in the chakras = a person growing = CONSCIOUSNESS EXPANDING.

On the other hand, a person "stuck" in a rut of fears, anger, and jealousy = the person's consciousness is CONTRACTING, and no growth happens during this phase.

Once the "shift" has happened, the consciousness of that person will be continually expanding, and the person will be in continual growth.

This is how the entire Universe operates, on the principles of expansion and contraction. And ultimately ALL of this requires the Grace of the Divine.

82

GOD'S WILL IS ALL THERE IS ~

All there is = god's will, as there is no such thing as free will ~

It is a simple shift in perception, of consciousness, to realize god's will precedes ALL, precedes all things great and small, for this = merging with god's consciousness, "uniting" with the all that is ~

For where there is no will of the "I", Divine consciousness is all that there is, as a flow of energy, one FIELD of Grace flowing through, and "inter"-acting with THE FIELD of Grace all around, in the web of oneness and energy which connects and bonds all things great and small together, in the perfect balance of expansion and contraction of the universe, the ebb and flow of growth and acceleration.

When god's will is all there is, there is no need to surrender, or succumb, it just "is", plain and simple, where Divine consciousness is all that exists. With this shift of perception, Divine will IS the only will = god realization. No thing could ever exist BUT god's will. It is all so simple and easy to SEE. The Grace of the Divine brings this shift in perception and this = god's will, plain and simple where surrendering is the natural state~

God's will is always flowing, at which point surrender IS the experience, succumbing IS the experience, dissolving IS the experience ~ it is all effortless, it cannot be cultivated or practiced, it just IS, god's will has completely taken over you ~

83

DIVINE COMMUNION ~

THE GOLDEN AGE _IS_ THE AGE OF DIVINE COMMUNION ~

The human perception and neural pathways in the brain are being activated by the cosmic consciousness, the Avataric consciousness right now, bringing the experience and full realization of the Divine to mankind. This type of communion has been missing for thousands and thousands of years for mankind. To experience the gross separation from the Divine, from god, has been mankind's journey.

Only the few, the saints and sages, here and there, could experience Divine communion on a regular basis. And NOW, as the Golden Age descends on us in this year 2012, this is to be had by ALL of mankind.

The Divine Presence is descending into collective consciousness of man first, and then coming into the individual consciousness. And it is descending swiftly and rapidly, for THIS IS THE TIME NOW. There is nothing else like it, this descent of the Divine into mankind!

So Divine communion will be completely unique to each individual and depends on the bond one has with the Divine. This is where maximum external effort has to be done by the individual. This is where the human MUST be empowered, to create a never-ending evolving and morphing bond with their Divine. For god is dependent on the devotee, in every way. This is how it is based on Universal Spiritual Laws. Mankind must initiate contact first, then god responds a thousand-fold.

~ DIVINE COMMUNION IS TO BE HAD BY ALL ~

What a glorious time to be ALIVE; to witness and participate in this great shift of the ages! Dancing and singing in praise and glory to the Divine activates the response from the Divine. Of course in all of the ancient and indigenous cultures, this IS how Divine communion works. And now this Divine communion, these tools to bond with the Divine, are being brought to the planet on a mass scale through Deeksha and the Oneness processes worldwide. Millions upon millions of everyday, normal people worldwide are experiencing the descent of the Divine into their lives, in a very real and very powerful way.

THIS DIVINE PHENOMENON IS REAL ~

IT IS HERE NOW ~

84

LIFE IS A MIRACLE ~

LIFE IS A MIRACLE

LIFE AS A MIRACLE

LIFE IS *THE* MIRACLE

Life is simply a series of miracles, one after the other, of Divine orchestration "behind the scenes". Once the shift is realized, then this orchestration is no longer hidden. The veil of illusion has dissolved, the illusion that there was a person there in the first place, has dissolved, and all that is left is the experience of pure Divine orchestration, of the ALL THAT IS ~

Because of the miraculous nature of life, ALL LIFE must be respected, revered, and honored. One form of life is not better than or above another form of life.

ALL LIFE IS THE MIRACULOUS PLAY OF THE DIVINE ~

ALL LIFE IS TO BE RESPECTED AND CHERISHED ~

THE INTERPLAY OF THE DIVINE

= "LIFE"

= "MAGIC"

= THE "MAGICAL LIFE"

THE MAGICAL LIFE IS ONE OF DIVINE GRACE,

ONE OF COMPLETE SURRENDER TO THE
DIVINE ~

85

MAN IS HEAVEN ON EARTH ~

THE DIVINE LED LIFE = THE MIRACULOUS LIFE

So why wouldn't you let the Divine in? That makes no sense of course, but it is the state of mankind right now. This is simply a fear-based projection.

So now we can sing and dance and rejoice in praise for this Divine filled life, for it is here NOW ~ Descending into millions of people across the planet. The gods are descending into mankind ~ this is not a myth, this is happening through a very real shift within the brain to people everywhere!

Mankind is becoming the "GODS", through this union of Heaven and Earth through the physical body, through this communion with the Divine. It is happening NOW, in this year of 2012 and beyond.

This is real; man IS becoming this god-link between heaven and earth. It is happening, are you ready? Is this what you want? It is **YOURS** to be had, this miraculous life of Grace. Simply pursue the bond with the Divine, this FIELD OF Grace all around you and inside of you.

86

SADHANA OF SEEING
THE MIRACLES ~

SEEING THE SYNCHRONICITIES IN YOUR LIFE

= WITNESSING THE DIVINE HAND IN LIFE

Of course, the nature of the Divine = coincidences, which really is another word for *synchronicities*. The web of oneness connects everything great and small.

1.) First STEP: you SEE the coincidences.
2.) Second STEP: You praise each and every synchronicity, because it is all so miraculous, of course!

LIFE IS MIRACULOUS

LIFE = MIRACLES

**SYNCHRONICITIES AND COINCIDENCES =
MIRACLES**

You praise by speaking the simple words of "thank you", for each and every synchronicity, every miracle, why? Because this **IS** the "ticket" to receiving more miracles. The bond with your Divine is so vitally important here. This conversation of "thank you" with your Divine initiates this bond, and then you are in the cycle of:

**SEEING, PRAISING, ASKING FOR MORE, AND
THEN RECEIVING MORE ~**

87

THE ONENESS TEMPLE ~

The Oneness Temple is an ACTIVATION CHAMBER, *activating the growth and expansion of human consciousness* ~ It is a massive structure, made out of marble. It is a living, breathing miracle of a Temple, and represents the womb of the descent of the Divine Presence into mankind. Man can come and sit and meditate and become activated into Awakening and God-Realization.

This structure is located at the Oneness University in India. It is beautiful and is a very powerful spot on the planet. This structure is to last throughout the Golden Age, the next 1000 years ~

It is located on very powerful grid lines (ley lines) of the planet, and acts like a POWERHOUSE GENERATOR OF AWAKENING for the entire human species.

THE ONENESS TEMPLE = AN ACTIVATION CHAMBER

Enjoy your time at Oneness University; this is the "place" to create *Super Soldiers of Light*. The Avataric consciousness will completely ACTIVATE you through Grace. Your time there = a Divine vacation with so many gifts to be bestowed on you ~

The Oneness University Campus + Oneness Temple

= AN INCUBATOR OF GRACE,

STABILIZING THE WHOLE PLANET INTO ONENESS CONSCIOUSNESS ~

PART 2

THE EXPERIENTIAL GUIDE
TO GRACE

Accessing THE FIELD through Deeksha

This section presents specific Teachings of Universal Truths and Laws as they relate to Awakening in the modern world ~ The Deeksha energy is transferred through these words of Grace, activating and initiating the "remembrance" of Awakening in our DNA ~

TWENTY-ONE TEACHINGS ~

WITH DEEKSHA INFUSED THROUGHOUT

EACH OF THESE TEACHINGS HAS AN AUDIO MEDITATION ~

TO ACCESS AUDIO MEDITATIONS, PLEASE VISIT:
WWW.WRITINGSFROMTHEONE.COM

"BOOK ONE, ONLINE"

PASSWORD: "Avatar Awakening"

THE FIELD of Grace is transferred through the written and spoken words of these Teachings ~

88

WHAT IS ONENESS?

What Is Oneness?
Law of One

WHAT IS ONENESS?
IT IS A LAW OF THE UNIVERSE
=
THE LAW OF ONENESS

- We are ALL "inter"-connected with ALL life.
- There is ONE consciousness that pervades ALL life, this is God Consciousness.
- This IS the natural order of the Universe.
- This IS life "inter"-acting in perfect coherence with ALL life.
- This IS existence, consciousness, bliss.

This Law of Oneness governs all the other Spiritual Laws of the Universe. Mankind MUST come back into *living in Oneness* for the survival of ALL life here on the planet. If mankind stays in a state of conflict, ALL life may be destroyed, including the human species. Now is the time for mankind to "wake up," to become *living in Oneness*.

These shifts of consciousness of Awakening and God-Realization bring the individual back into perfect coherence and living *within* all the Spiritual Laws of the Universe. This = the importance of the Oneness work!

One person *living in Oneness* naturally aligns one hundred thousand people around him to also be aligned with Oneness. This is how the Universe works: Law of Resonance (like attracts like). This is how Awakened and God-Realized Beings affect the whole morphogenic field of humanity!

The remembrance of "Oneness" is IN our DNA; it IS what calls us to the Oneness Phenomenon and Oneness Work, in whatever capacity we are involved in ~ whether we are a Trainer, Deeksha Giver, or Deeksha Receiver. *Living in Oneness* is our natural state, our birthright. When an individual *lives in Oneness,* the natural progression is then to SHARE Oneness to others, and then to uphold and protect Oneness and the Oneness work.

Enormous positive Karma is generated by those working within the Laws of Oneness and actively promoting Oneness and upholding the Oneness work.

89

THE NATURE OF THE
DIVINE PRESENCE ~

The Nature of the Divine Presence
"Remembrances" located in our DNA

THE DIVINE PRESENCE **IS**:

- A FIELD.
- An interactive FIELD.
- A tangible and accessible FIELD of Grace.
- Infinitely abundant and "Grace"-ious.
- A FIELD *dependent* on us.

These ARE *remembrances* located in our DNA, being activated now through these words of Grace, during this current "shift of the ages." It is up to man to activate THIS FIELD from our end, it is our responsibility, and "this" must be remembered.

We, as empowered individuals, must step up to the plate. We must take action and activate THE FIELD. This = the Universal Spiritual "Law of Action."

How does one do this?

1.) First and foremost, one must **recognize** THE FIELD, **acknowledge** THE FIELD, and **praise** THE FIELD. Praise is the very simple yet powerful action of giving "thanks" and acknowledging *everything* THE FIELD gives us on a minute-by-minute basis. Praise IS speaking the words: "thank you," both internally and externally.

THE FIELD outside + all around us = the same FIELD of Grace inside us. It is the sense of "I" that literally blocks this recognition. Once the shift of Awakening and God-Realization happens, the "I" dissolves and all that is left is this recognition of pure Presence "BEING" this Divine vehicle of Grace.

This physical body = the god-link between heaven and earth. Pure Presence stares out of the eyes and "is" the driver of "this life."

2.) The second way to activate THE FIELD is to consciously ask to be this god-link, to be the Divine vehicle of Grace. This action = man reaching out to god. It is time NOW for humans all around the planet to be this link, to connect heaven + earth through the physical body with god consciousness. This = the "missing link" right now, the "god link."

Fortunately for all of us, we have processes from the Oneness University to get directly linked and bonded with our Presence. For those who have passion and are willing to take action and put in external effort: Grace WILL deliver, for this IS the nature of the Universe.

3.) The third way to activate THE FIELD of Divine Presence is to create and cultivate a relationship with THE FIELD. This is absolutely necessary! Give it a name, give it a form, give it a personality and a role (e.g., a best friend, a Divine mother, a Divine father). Spend time throughout the day actively cultivating this relationship, for it IS very ALIVE and must be treated as such. Put in maximum effort, the rewards are infinite ~

In closing, this IS our role on the planet now, to consciously and actively reach out to the Divine Presence utilizing all the gifts of the spiritual Laws of the Universe. Putting in maximum effort = maximum response from god. Grace will deliver.

90

IS AWAKENING AND GOD-REALIZATION IMPORTANT?

Is Awakening and God-Realization Important? Of Course
Law of Resonance

Once the shift of Awakening happens to an individual, the sense of "self" dissolves. What is left are various personalities arising and falling when needed. So the "ego games" have ended, the suffering deemed "personal" has ceased, and an enormous energy has been freed up! You see: the "attachment to the mind" consumes so much energy, so much "life force" to sustain the "ego" and the "games." Suffering actually consumes so much life force. Of course, this is how it is all sustained. So once the neurobiological shift of Awakening occurs through Grace, a rush of energy is then released.

When there is no longer a sense of "I," resistance transmutes into acceptance. Then the individual ceases "controlling" everyone and everything, and ceases being the active "do"-er. What remains is a life lived without the "interference of the mind." So the individual can just "be" and just experience reality as it is, without resistance or trying to change it. A deep peace, silence, and sense of calm pervade.

As the journey of Awakening continues, and the individual shifts into "realizing god," walking with god, and talking with god, then the individual sees that he is purely a vehicle of "god," of Divine Grace, of pure Presence. The individual "sees" god in all others, all things, all events, all creatures, and in all nature. The needs of a "self" have ceased because a sense of self has dissolved. Now, only the sense of "Presence" exists, so naturally the individual is aligned with a much higher purpose and vision of the planet and cosmos.

The individual is infused with "god consciousness," within the billions of cells of his being. This = *an enormous amount of energy* = *"god energy,"* that propels the "physical self" through life, being the "god-link" between heaven and earth. So the importance of all this is that this individual is now the "physical link" of god energy, connecting heaven and earth, walking the planet as this god-link wherever he goes.

This god-link = an enormous LIGHTHOUSE, literally filled and resonating with Avataric Light and Oneness Consciousness within THE FIELD all around him. This individual affects THE FIELD all around him, this = the Law of Resonance. The Law of Resonance states that all things are vibration of energy, and like attracts like. So the vibration of this god-realized individual affects ALL life and consciousness around him, naturally and automatically working in harmony with the Universal Spiritual Laws. Others around him will very naturally be "lifted up." This = the only way for man to lift up mankind around him, by being this "ONE" god-link.

Now just imagine many thousands of these "god-links" walking the planet. What happens naturally = a coherence within ALL life around these people ~ coherence with people, animals, nature, weather patterns, and so on. So natural catastrophes will be averted, global uprisings either cease or become diffused, harmony will pervade. All these god-realized "lighthouses" connect together around the planet into a huge web of Light, Grace, and Oneness: naturally raising the Resonance of all mankind and life.

Remember, you are ALL here to be the god-link between heaven and earth. The Universe is infinitely rich and abundant with magic and gifts. The Universe organizes itself within the Spiritual Laws of the Universe. Mankind must SEE and use these Laws as "gifts" to consciously and actively initiate global coherence on the planet. DEEKSHA is the Divine energy that fuels these Laws. Once the shifts of Awakening and God-Realization have occurred, the individual will be living within harmony of all these Universal Laws, thus *LIVING IN ONENESS* with ALL around him.

Note: All the Spiritual Universal Laws work together and in balance. One cannot be utilized without affecting the other. Some examples of these Laws are Law of Resonance, Law of One, Law of Attraction, Law of Action.

91

GOD IS DEPENDENT ON THE DEVOTEE ~

God Is Dependent on the Devotee
Law of Action

During this teaching, I use the term "god" interchangeably with the terms "Divine Presence" and "FIELD of Grace." This is how I personally relate to the "All That IS." Please use any word or words that you feel comfortable with when relating to your own Divinity. Please use any form of god or Universal Energy that you are comfortable with.

"Devotee" means mankind, the individual, all of us.

This teaching, "God is Dependent on the Devotee," is based on a Universal Spiritual Law. There are many such Spiritual Laws that the Universe operates on, and they affect all life and consciousness. This Law is the Universal Law of Action.

The Law of Action states that we must move in the direction of our desires in order to achieve them. We must engage in some action that supports what we think about and dream about.

Man MUST first take action in **ANY** area of life. This is true within the business world, within relationships, within health, and *especially* within spiritual growth and Awakening.

TAKING ACTION
= DIRECTLY "INTER"-ACTING WITH THE FIELD
OF GRACE ~

For example, this is true in the business world. If you just graduated from business school with an MBA, and it was your intention to start your own successful business, you would take action. You would take *every* step necessary to align your new business for success, would you not? Of course you would! You would put in the maximum external effort required, and you would do this consciously, and hopefully with passion. Ultimately, the success that comes in with this external effort is abundance through Grace, so this abundant success = the Universe responding to your "action."

So when we desire any spiritual growth, Awakening, and God-Realization, it is the same Universal Law of Action that is at work. When we desire these things, we have to reach out to the Universe first. It is a Universal Law: man must reach out to god first, to initiate contact. It cannot happen any other way. This is how the "game" of being "human" was structured eons ago. How this game was structured is incredibly complex, not to go into now. However, how THE FIELD of Grace is designed can be explained.

THIS FIELD IS ALL PERVASIVE, OMNIPRESENT, EVERYWHERE THROUGH TIME AND SPACE.

IT IS EXISTENCE, CONSCIOUSNESS, BLISS.

SATCHITANANDA PARABRAMHA.

This is the first line of the Oneness University's sacred mantra in Sanskrit: "The Moolamantra". THIS FIELD of Grace is in every single cell of our being, connecting and "inter"-acting with THE FIELD of Grace all around.

So man being here on Earth is playing the game; man agreed to come to Earth to feel the complete sense of separation from the Divine. This is what we ALL signed up to do, ALL of us alive today, to feel and experience this separation from god. This **IS** the human game.

However, there is a "REMEMBERANCE," amongst all of us, especially those involved in the Oneness Work, at whatever capacity we are involved in, whether we are a Trainer, Deeksha Giver, or Deeksha Receiver. This "remembrance" is of "Oneness," the Law of Oneness, which is another Universal Spiritual Law. This remembrance is in our DNA and is what calls us to the Oneness Phenomenon, whether we are conscious of it or not. This has been located in our DNA through all our various lifetimes and dimensional lineages.

So NOW, as we are participating in the greatest shift of the ages mankind has ever been able to participate in, it is time for the "Wake Up." It is time for Awakening and God-Realization.

How is this happening NOW? Man **MUST** set the action into motion. It **MUST** be initiated by man. Man **MUST** reach out to god and initiate the link between Heaven and Earth. Man **MUST** ask to be this "god-link." This is how to activate and initiate THE FIELD of Grace into motion for Spiritual Growth, Awakening, and God-Realization.

How does one initiate this? On a very basic level, man must *acknowledge* the Divine on a daily basis, ideally throughout the whole day. Acknowledging is the very simple yet powerful ACT OF PRAISING the Divine for absolutely everything in one's life. This is not the same as invoking gratitude; this is simply PRAISE.

PRAISE is the conscious act of speaking words of "thanks" internally or out loud externally to your god and Divinity for everything. Everything, whether it is termed as pleasant or unpleasant, needs to be praised, for it is all the Divine hand in one's life. There is a certain vibration created by this "Act of Praise." This vibration = the same vibration as THE FIELD of Grace. You can think of praise as speaking "the same language of the Divine Universe."

What does praise sound like? It is so easy, and I feel it is one of the most important sadhanas (spiritual practice) to consciously engage in all day. It is simply to say to your Divine, "I praise you Divine Presence," and then list the things that are happening to you during the day. Praise all the people who are around you and cross your path throughout the day: all your family members, work colleagues, even strangers, for each and every one of these are the Divine helping you with your day and life's journey. Praise all nature and animals, everything. Praise as things are happening, and also praise during a meditation, at the beginning of the day or at the end of the day. If you want to spend ten or fifteen minutes writing the praise down in a journal, it will be so very effective.

This question is asked all the time: "Well, if Grace is the only thing that has the power to awaken me, then why should I put in any external effort at all?"

BECAUSE, this is how the Universe is structured ~ It is structured on this very important LAW OF ACTION ~ Man must put in maximum external effort for anything he desires in life, especially Awakening!

True ~ Grace IS the only thing capable of Awakening an individual, to give that shift of consciousness. However, man must initiate the connection with god first through maximum external effort. There are infinite ways to reach out to god; there are seven billion people on the planet, we will all have our own unique way. However, here are some general examples to put this Universal Law of Action into motion:

- Praise, the act of acknowledging the Divine all day long.
- Prayer and meditation.
- Sadhanas, which are spiritual practices; examples are any of the practices within the Oneness Community: 64-Deeksha, Mukthi Deeksha, Oneness Bhakti Yoga, receiving Deeksha, and the Oneness Meditation.
- Seva, which is selfless service to mankind. One of the most important acts of seva on the planet is to help mankind awaken, and of course within the Oneness Community, this is through giving Deeksha and facilitating the advanced processes.

All these acts = mankind reaching out to god, initiating contact with the Divine.

These Universal Principles apply to wherever you are on the spiritual path, whether you are completely new to all this, or you have had many shifts into higher consciousness, or anywhere in between.

Maximum external effort results in maximum response from god. It is a never-ending process, your bond with the Divine grows, evolves, and morphs every day! Your bond with the Divine is a symbiotic relationship, which means your Divine depends on YOU as much as YOU depend on your Divine! This actually creates great empowerment for the individual. On the other hand, waiting for Grace your whole life without initiating contact first or without putting in maximum effort actually creates great disempowerment. What we need now on the planet are empowered humans consciously and actively reaching out to the Divine. The results are extraordinary! Imagine seven billion people on the planet right now, all actively and consciously reaching out to god; THIS IS HEAVEN ON EARTH ~

In closing, all life in the Universe utilizes "THE FIELD of Grace" constantly and consistently, which = the forward motion of LIFE. All species utilize THIS FIELD in perfect coherence. Mankind, however, is the only species as a whole right now NOT utilizing the Laws of the Universe consciously and in the proper way, thus unconsciously creating all of the external incoherent experiences existing today. Mankind must remember these important Laws of the Universe and how to utilize them in a proper way for the benefit of all life.

So please let us all utilize the Law of Action to become successful in all areas of our life: to be a good businessman, to be in fulfilling relationships, to have a healthy body, to give back to the planet, and to be on the Awakening journey, to walk toward god, and to walk WITH god.

92

ONLY THE GOD-BOND CAN BRING A SENSE OF COMPLETION TO AN INDIVIDUAL ~

Only the God-Bond Can Bring a Sense of "Completion" to an Individual
The God-Bond Is the "Key" to Life

The search for anything else for a "sense of completion" is an illusion, a falsehood, a game of the mind. People are in constant search for this in relationships, material wealth, events and activities, and in physical satisfaction (eating, sex, exercise) ~ in infinite ways in fact. No one and no thing can ever bring a sense of "completion" to an individual. Only the God-Bond will bring this ~ this bond of walking with god, talking with god, and the infinite "discovery" of god.

The Presence **IS** the only "Presence" one should be striving to have a relationship with for this "sense of completion." Once this shift of the "God Bond" has occurred, the individual can then fully enjoy all other relationships with maximum fulfillment ~ Why? Because he is no longer seeking from and having expectations from another that *only* the Presence can deliver. This = freedom and true liberation ~ This is being FREE from the bondage of relationships.

The extreme isolation and intense loneliness felt by humans at this time on the planet is simply due to the "sense of separation" from god. Once this is recognized with awareness as being the "root cause" of one's own suffering, then one can actively and consciously cultivate a relationship with the Divine, utilizing the Universal Spiritual Laws (e.g., the Law of Action). Man must reach out to the Divine first. The Divine will respond accordingly.

Once the shift has occurred, the individual then fully accepts "what is" about the other in relationships, whether it is a spouse, romantic partner, father, mother, or child. Any resistance has been transmuted into *acceptance*, even full acceptance of the other! What does acceptance mean? ACCEPT-ING ALL GRACE IN ~ this takes on the form of joy, bliss, ecstasy, love, peace, calm, and oneness. Why? Because resistance no longer exists!

Just imagine right now, for a moment, being with your partner and *accepting* everything about that person ~ all traits, emotions, habits, charges, so-called "shortcomings," physical looks, past behavior ~ everything. Well, it actually is a reality, it is exquisite! It is mankind's true nature, to be experiencing others in relationships like this! Awakening is truly experiencing the "what is" in the other.

This experience is descending rapidly on the planet right now, through the consciousness shifts of Awakening and God-Realization. Once these shifts have occurred, the experiential realization exists that your partner is *pure* Divine essence in all his manifestations: through his words, actions, deeds, profession, eyes, and heart. The terms "good traits" versus "bad traits" no longer exist, for ALL traits are pure god essence, pure Divine Presence. This happens within all of your relationships, as a natural progression, automatically, effortlessly, driven by Grace, as it is our true nature.

Being in complete communion with our god is our birthright! One only has to be aware of this and to then actively cultivate the relationship with the Presence for the Presence to deliver this God—Bond.

In closing, it is of utmost importance to *"remember"* that this God-Bond is VERY real and VERY accessible. It is not a myth. It is no longer JUST for the aesthetics, the monks, the ones living in spiritual seclusion. Quite the contrary, in fact. It is for ALL, here and now ~ for all of us living in the modern world, in the West, in the material realm ~ as we live with partners and families, work in the corporate world, with bills to pay, as doctors, lawyers, bankers, all professions ~ The Divine Presence is descending within mankind, right now, during this great shift of the ages; it is our birthright! Please remember to put your relationship with the Divine first and foremost. Cultivate this relationship throughout the day, every single day ~ The rewards are infinite!

93

DISTRACTIONS: WALKING AND TALKING WITH GOD IN THE MODERN WORLD ~

DISTRACTIONS: Walking and Talking with God in the Modern World
The Law of Attraction

There are so many modern day distractions, especially in the Western world, created by the sense of "I" to keep the Presence and voice of god far away. Walking and talking with god in the modern world, amidst all the distractions ~ this **IS** our way ~ There is no other way for us, for we are not monks, not ascetics. We in fact lead very complex and busy lives with families, companies, jobs, and bills to pay.

The distractions are endless ~ an example is the excessive amount of "noise" generated in our society from radios, televisions, games, traffic, construction, people, planes, trains, and cell phones. Another example is the distractions generated by the media: images and video from magazines, advertisements, billboards, newspapers, books, movies, computers, and on televisions.

The sense of "I" loves distractions; why? Because the distractions all give the "I" survival, a very long life. As long as one is surrounded and attached to distractions, the search to know god and cultivate a relationship and bond with the Divine will be very small indeed. It can be seen as an equation:

WRITINGS FROM THE ONE

~THE MORE ONE SEEKS DISTRACTIONS, THE LESS ONE SEEKS TO KNOW GOD ~

~THE MORE ONE SEEKS GOD, THE LESS ONE SEEKS DISTRACTIONS ~

Simple as that. This is based on the Universal Law of Attraction: "Whatever you shall seek, you shall find." What you seek, thus putting your attention and focus on, you shall find. So it makes obvious sense: the more one seeks distractions, the more one will find distractions. The more one seeks to know the Divine, the more one finds the Divine.

So the question is: how to navigate all the distractions in this modern world we live in?

Answer: to commune with god at maximum flow and potential, it takes focus and dedication, so it is always best to remove yourself from distractions, of course ~ Go to where there is the least amount of distractions for you. Perhaps in nature, of course! In the absolute exquisite silent Presence of nature, away from the noise of man-made distractions. Alive with pure and unadulterated nature, teeming with LIFE, lakes, rivers, forests, bees, birds, fish, breezes, clouds, sun, dragonflies, ants, dirt, flowers, trees ~ all exquisite in their Presence. The voices of nature, singing and dancing in praise to the Divine all around!

Remember, empowered individuals make choices toward the direction they want their life to head in. They make choices all day long, saying "YES" and "NO" loudly and clearly. What do you say YES to on a daily basis? What are you saying NO to? Take a minute to reflect on this.

Are you saying YES to:

1.) Distractions?
2.) Television, magazines, newspapers?
3.) Mindless shopping?
4.) Idle chatter/gossip?

Or, are you saying YES to:

1.) Contemplation?
2.) Meditation?
3.) Cultivating your relationship with your Divine?
4.) Connecting with Grace through the giving/receiving of Deeksha?
5.) Actively reaching out to god?

Are you saying NO to:

1.) Social standards?
2.) Status quo?
3.) Old paradigms?
4.) Fear-based actions?
5.) Untruths told by others?

Or are you saying NO to:

1.) Quiet time?
2.) Solitude?
3.) Time in nature?
4.) Putting external effort in communing with your god?
5.) Realizing god, for example, through the Oneness Processes?

Just "SEE" what and who you are saying YES and NO to ~

Just "SEE" and realize these choices are attracting your present and future to you.

Are you seeking a life of distraction? Or are you seeking a life of Awakening and God-Realization? You will know the answer; Grace is delivering the answers to you now.

What we need now are empowered individuals, consciously and actively making decisions on a daily basis (ideally all day long) that bring god to them and through them, to be walking and talking with god. You decide ~ what do you want?

94

GOD'S WILL VS. FREE WILL ~

GOD'S WILL VS. FREE WILL

There is no such thing as "free will"; that is simply an illusion created by the sense of "I" ~ "God's will" is all there is. "God's will" is all there has ever been ~ we are just "vehicles of Divine Grace."

Before the shifts of Awakening and God-Realization, the "I" claims control of one's life and destiny, and that is why there is a constant struggle internally. After the shifts of Awakening and God-Realization, all that is left **IS GOD** and **GOD'S WILL** working through the body. This becomes an experiential realization and happens automatically. It is exquisite ~

Life is meant to be "god filled" and "god led." It is only the severe sense of separation that has created such a strong sense of "I." This "I" is actually creating insanity for mankind ~ it **IS** a form of madness. You see, as long as there is a sense of "I," there will be the incessant internal struggle, the constant mind chatter, the "I" questioning the voice of god and "trying" to control one's destiny. This of course is one of the biggest illusions mankind is experiencing. The existence of the concept of "free will," and the right and glorification of free will

= THE BIG ILLUSION ~

Realizing "god's will" is just that ~ an experiential reality after the shifts of Awakening and God-Realization have occurred.

Until that point, this will remain just a concept. This breakdown of the "I" is happening, and happening rapidly worldwide. Let's take the West for example ~ what you are seeing now in the West **IS** the breakdown of the "I." How is this manifesting in the external world? Well, very clearly you can see it through various ways:

- **System and institution breakdowns** ~ The restructuring of the banking, mortgage, and real estate industries, to name a few.
- **Psychological breakdowns** ~ People are literally going mad, unable to cope, and suicide is increasing.
- **Weather patterns** ~ These will continue to increase in erratic patterns in the near future and cause havoc for mankind.
- **Physical body breakdown** ~ Such things as deadly strokes and heart attacks are happening to more people, and at a much earlier age.

Avataric Consciousness has entered the planet's consciousness and **IS** breaking down the "I" in all ways. It is all part of the <u>BIRTH</u> of the Golden Age, of the "new man," of society based on the higher consciousness. It is actually such a beautiful process when witnessed from the "bird's eye view." Institutions and thought-forms based on the old "fear-based" paradigm are being broken apart. This HAS to happen, to house the new consciousness. So remember to rejoice! Sing and dance when these manifestations occur within us and within the collective experience of mankind:

~ FOR IT IS ALL THE DIVINE HAND AT WORK ~

95

"BE"-ING AT ONE WITH
THE UNIFIED FIELD ~

"BE"-ING AT ONE WITH THE UNIFIED FIELD
The Universal Law of Oneness

Oneness with God

= Oneness with the Universe

= Be-ing at ONE with the Universal Laws

= Be-ing at ONE with the Universal Processes

= ONE with the Unified Field

~EVERYTHING IN THE UNIVERSE IS "IN PROCESS"~

The Unified Field is a "dance" of cosmic interaction, of god-energy weaving its way through every particle of the Universe. Humans, as a whole, are the only species on the planet not at ONE with the Unified Field. This is because the nature of the "I" (the sense of separate self) causes severe separation and energy disruption from god.

This = a very sad existence = a life for true warriors!

You all signed up for this "separate"-tion from god. To journey into this lifetime IS FOR TRUE WARRIORS. Why? Because the human experience right now is a type of hell ~ hell simply means "being separate from god."

THE SHIFTS OF AWAKENING AND GOD-REALIZATION AUTOMATICALLY TRANSMUTE THIS HELL INTO HEAVEN ON EARTH ~

THIS = A MAGICAL GARDEN OF EDEN, OF INFINITE POSSIBILITIES.

The Universal Laws are the keys to this HEAVEN ON EARTH. NOW is the time to unlock the mysteries of the Universe. These cogs in the wheels of the Universe must be unlocked NOW for the empowerment of all humans, which thus = the survival of mankind.

All other creatures and life are at ONE with the Unified Field. All one has to do is be still in nature and observe ~ NOW is the time for mankind to be at ONE with the Unified Field ~ In fact, it MUST happen. Man must start utilizing the Universal Laws for the benefit of all life in Oneness and harmony.

Being the god-link, thus being at ONE with the Unified Field, **IS** the purpose of this life. The Oneness Phenomenon plays a very specific role on the planet, because each individual at ONE with god = a stabilizing force during this shift. Nothing in the exterior world can disturb this stabilizing force.

The Tree of Life extends up through Mother Earth through humans, reaching up to the heavens and becoming the god-link. Humans are the limbs of this Tree of Life. Mother Earth is birthing the new race of humans, these god-links, with grounding support from Gaia (Mother Earth) in prefect balance with the Cosmic Energy from the Sun. Humans are the "god-link" between heaven and earth.

GAIA + HUMANS AS THE GOD-LINK + SUN

= "HEAVEN ON EARTH" ~

What is Heaven on Earth? A perceptual shift, where ONE sees the Divine in everything and is in complete acceptance of it all~

~ WHERE THERE IS NO RESISTANCE, THERE IS ONENESS~

Nothing has to change in the outer world, nothing ~ the perceptual shift happens internally, then naturally affects the outer world. The inner perceptual shift happens first for an individual, then this person walks the planet as "Heaven on Earth," directly affecting all life around this person and through time and space. THE FIELD is forever transmuted by this vibration. So people, places, things, and even *events* are forever transmuted into the higher frequency of ONENESS.

Deeksha is the energetic tool to connect mankind to the Unified Field of Grace and Oneness. This tool is used over and over until the shifts of Awakening and God-Realization have occurred.

TO BE AT ONE WITH THE UNIFIED FIELD _IS_ THE GREATEST SERVICE (SEVA) TO THE PLANET

TO BE EMPOWERED

= TO BE IN POWER, IN POWER WITH THE UNIVERSE~

The Universe empowers humans, as humans reach out to god first.

Be-ing at ONE with the Unified Field = resonating at the same frequency THE FIELD resonates at = a very high frequency!

That is why so much shifting must happen in the physical body and all the koshas (energy bodies).

All the koshas must be cleansed and balanced for the god-energy to take permanent residence. This is why sadhanas for all the various koshas are so important, then Grace has direct access to bring the shifts of Awakening and God-Realization ~ Please utilize the Divine gifts of Deeksha and all of the Oneness processes, as these are some of the most powerful sadhanas on the planet for accelerated Awakening and God-Realization ~

96

CHARGES WITH OTHERS REFLECT THE UNSEEN AND UNACCEPTED ASPECTS OF OURSELVES ~

Charges with Others Reflect the Unseen and Unaccepted Aspects of Ourselves
The Law of Resonance

Charges = Energy, so another person's actions and qualities can cause charges in you; why? Because their behavior is *resonating* a certain energetic frequency within you, thus equaling *"the charge."* This person is actually resonating back to you the exact same resonating energy inside **YOU.**

- It **IS** a Blessing.
- It **IS** Exquisite.
- This person **IS** a "mirror" for you.

So take each and every opportunity to "look" into your charges when they arise; make it a "lesson." It actually becomes a very fun lesson, because god consciousness is here to "show" you exactly what this person is mirroring. Call out to the Divine, for god is dependent on the devotee. When examining this "issue" with another, ask, *"What have I NOT seen or accepted about myself?"*

THIS = REALIZATION ~

God will show you. There are major charges, which = massive emotions, such as: anger, jealousy, rage. There are also minor charges, such as annoyance and irritation. A charge is a charge is a charge is a charge ~ they will vary in degree, of course! It all depends on the "energy" associated with this charge and how "repressed" it is.

The sense of "I" will try to blame the other as being "at fault." This **IS** the role of the "I," to protect it! However, this is only an illusion. The "I" can never "figure" out the true nature of a charge; only the Grace of the Divine will bestow this as a self-realization.

Once the shifts of Awakening and God-Realization have occurred, the "I" is dissolved, and only pure god consciousness exists, then the process of "seeing" the charge, experiencing the charge, and processing the charge becomes effortless and natural; it happens very quickly.

The charge*:*

- **Is Seen.**
- **Is Experienced.**
- **Burns off.**
- **Transmutes into joy and bliss.**
- **Transmutes into peace and calm.**

~ ALL THROUGH GRACE: IT IS EFFORTLESS ~

Through NO effort of "our own" can this occur. Surrender, helplessness, and humility to the Grace of god are the natural byproducts of Awakening and God-Realization. These qualities naturally lead to zero resistance to *"what is,"* thus to the charge.

When there is no resistance, the charge is able to express itself fully as a form of energy moving through the various koshas. This = fully experiencing the charge (i.e., physically, emotionally, spiritually). The shift of Awakening = the koshas are properly cleansed and balanced, thus facilitating the "easy processing" of a charge.

Just SEE how "your relationships are your greatest gurus," for this = Universal Spiritual Law of *The Law of Resonance*.

Do not be afraid of charges ~ SEE them as your greatest teacher ~

Utilize god consciousness to process them. This all comes back to the importance of cultivating your relationship and bond with the Divine on a daily basis, for it is only this God-Bond that will bring you self-realization. SEE the process as a game if you will, a fun and humbling game. Westerners are very "goal-oriented"; we thrive on challenges! So take this as your personal challenge ~ to face your charges head on. Do not run from them, for they will only follow you and intensify! The sooner you face them, the better. The "clearings" are happening so very, very rapidly now for mankind ~ this must be rejoiced!

In closing, the times are on us NOW ~ to rapidly transmute charges, transform, and move into much higher awareness and consciousness such as Awakening and God-Realization. The gifts of Grace are so infinitely abundant during this unique "window of opportunity," as we are in these years of the *"Great Shift of the Ages"* ~

Utilize ALL these gifts. The Universe **IS** bestowing all THESE on mankind NOW ~ Utilize the gifts of Deeksha and the Oneness processes, for these greatly "accelerate" the seeing, experiencing, and processing of charges. Face the challenges head on ~ the rewards are infinite!

97

FREEDOM FROM RELATIONSHIPS ~

FREEDOM FROM RELATIONSHIPS

God's Grace flows through all beings, all creatures great and small, plants, mountains, rivers, wind, and sky, in this glorious cycle of oneness. There is no one to "control" anything, just a witnessing to the magnificence of god's Grace, THE FIELD of Grace working in perfect balance and harmony. How could anyone think they have "control"? Ah, the greatest illusion of the separate mind ~

TO ALLOW = The Law of Allowance ~

TO ACCEPT = The Law of Acceptance ~

These are the Laws of god consciousness, of THE FIELD of Grace. What a glorious existence to realize the Grace of god, the hand of Grace in all things.

How could there ever be "free will"? This is such an illusion that the ego loves to replicate over and over, in these *ego games*. Thus the reason for the dramas here on planet Earth. The "I" is stuck in ego games, in self-destructive patterns of "energy manipulations." Rise above only through the Grace of god. No "I" can ever rise above these ego games, only a sheer act of Divine Grace can bring these shifts to realize these ego games at play and to be FREE ~

EGO GAMES = SURVIVALIST TACTICS

Of course! How else can the ego survive? Where god exists, the ego dies ~ the ego is so very threatened by this god consciousness ~ Just SEE those around you, see who are stuck in these ego games. The more they are surrounded by the sheer Grace of god, the more their ego rises up to dominate ~ Just SEE in the drama.

The Grace of god is here for everyone; will everyone accept it? Of course not ~ As more access to god consciousness is available on the planet right now during this portal of 2012-2014, the more the ego will rise up, of course! In perfect duality, all in the dance of energy, a beautiful balancing act ~

Only god consciousness rises above all this. There is only ONE existence now, being at ONE with god consciousness, where all drama dissolves immediately, all karma played out, and energies released forever, in a cut of energy that Grace provides. All those engaging in ego games drop away in a very accelerated rate ~ god consciousness takes care of all this.

FREEDOM FROM RELATIONSHIPS

= FREEDOM FROM THE BONDAGE OF RELATIONSHIPS ~

THE CLUCTHES OF THE MIND = THE CLUTCHES OF RELATIONSHIPS ~

True FREEDOM comes when only god remains, and life becomes an interplay of Divine consciousness through all beings, all creatures great and small, within perfect balance and harmony of all the Universal Laws and principles. How lucky are we to realize this? This bondage creates such suffering for humans; how can anyone be fulfilled in a relationship when the clutches of the mind create bondage? There truly can't be ~ only realizing god consciousness frees one from this bondage, in one giant ACT OF

GRACE. TRUE FREEDOM THEN PREVAILS WHEN ALL
THAT IS LEFT IS THE DIVINE ~

These bondages of relationships are all necessary, of course, and
= the Divine human play of existence on planet Earth. This has
all been the dance for thousands of years and simply equals one
existence of the human experience.

Now, however, during this great shift of the ages, the Grace of
god is fully accessible to break these bondages once and for all
~ this IS A REALITY, this IS HAPPENING to people all over
the world.

NOW ~ imagine a planet of seven billion people all FREE from
these bondages ~ this would create heaven on earth for all indeed.
Heaven on earth = god consciousness fully taking over, releasing
the bondages of the mind, thus = freedom within all relationships.
So the question is, do you choose this heaven on earth?

98

THE CARDINAL RULE OF RELATIONSHIPS ~

THE CARDINAL RULE OF RELATIONSHIPS
This is THE cardinal rule of relationships:

YOU ARE "ATTRACT"-ING ALL RELATIONSHIPS IN YOUR LIFE DUE TO THE "LAW OF RESONANCE" AND "THE LAW OF KARMA" ~

Very simply: "like attracts like"~

There is a massive clearing going on right now, all thanks to the extraordinary amounts of Grace available during this portal of 2012-2014. Take advantage of this! Do it consciously and "Grace"-FULLY ~ Lifetimes upon lifetimes of the "bondages of karma" one has accumulated can all be released right here, right now ~ all with the help of Grace, of course ~

Do the work, SEE what you have been attracting ~ SEE what games, dramas, and situations you yourself "attract." As one moves into higher vibrations at a dramatically accelerated pace, relationships and dramas will all be "released" at a rapid pace too ~ one cannot happen without the other.

It is very important to remember that as one utilizes this Avataric consciousness to awaken, grow, and transform, so much LIGHT is being infused into ALL of your energy bodies. Take your physical body, for example: the Avataric consciousness actually infuses the billions of cells of your being with higher consciousness, thus activating DNA, soul contracts, and "remembrances." This pure Avataric light has the power and capability to transform conditionings and thought patterns of the "old paradigm," which is based on fear and separation. It **IS** happening now, to people all across the planet!

This portal of 2012-2014 is so vitally important ~ there is a huge task at hand, and it has to happen to people like you.

~ DO IT NOW ~

~ DO IT GRACE-FULLY ~

Allow and accept all Grace to come into your life to awaken, grow, and transform. This is your task ~ Do you ever feel you are alone in this process, alone in your journey of all this clearing going on in your life, alone in all your relationships being reflected back to you in an accelerated way? Of course you do; however, please realize the "ONES" aligned with Avataric consciousness are ALL DOING THIS NOW ~

Yes, a "few" take on the task of the "many," this is how the morphogenic field *shifts* in exponential ways with ripple effects through time and space, and through all dimensions.

Please remember: **YOU** and only **YOU** are attracting "issues" in another for you to SEE, due to the law of "cause and effect" and the law of resonance.

For example, if there is fear, resistance, or anger in another, please SEE this = **<u>YOUR OWN</u>** fear, resistance, and anger.

Please remember:

LIFE IS RELATIONSHIP, AND YOU ARE ALL REFLECTING BACK TO EACH OTHER WHAT

YOU NEED TO "SEE, ACCEPT, AND HEAL" IN YOURSELVES ~

You SEEING what you need to in yourself will automatically "set right the relationship" with the other. It truly is as simple as that, and Grace **IS** absolutely needed for these realizations and processing ~ Utilize Deeksha and the Oneness processes to access the enormous amounts of Grace available to mankind right now ~

So rejoice with each other, that you all aligned this eons ago together, to experience this all right NOW, in this great shift of the ages ~

99

GOD CONSCIOUSNESS
IGNITES EGO GAMES ~

GOD CONSCIOUSNESS IGNITES EGO GAMES

The more god consciousness streaming in = the more those around you play ego games. "Ego games" is just another term for "energy games" and manipulation. This is within the natural Laws and principles of the Universe. After all, this perfect balance of the following occurs within all life and consciousness:

- Expansion/Contraction
- Ebb/Flow
- Growing/Dying
- Moving Forward/Moving Backwards

God consciousness flows to and through individuals ~ the consciousness springs through, out, and all around, inviting and encouraging expansion and growth in all it comes in contact with. Those not willing to grow or expand with this consciousness actually do not "resonate" with it ~ so instead of resonating at the same high frequency, the ego's only tactic is "DEFENSIVENESS." To be DEFENSIVE = survival mode.

Instead of "growing with god's Grace," the person resists god's Grace in a contraction of energies, shutting down completely and actually resisting growth or SEEING ~

Ego games rise up in so many ways:

- Trying to start drama and engage others in drama ~
- The need for attention ~
  This "need for attention" = BOREDOM = the mind is fully engaged and overactive, ruling a person's life. It actually indicates very low kundalini and is the state of the majority of mankind right now ~
- Complaining about another ~
  This = complete defensiveness, to make one's ego feel better. Ultimately everything that is being complained about is simply a reflection of oneself ~
- The need to control another and the need to have ownership over another ~

These ego games simply indicate a "severe separation from god," separation from the ALL THAT IS. This type of drama from another is futile when ONE is free from the bondages of relationships, meaning there is no charge in you to interplay with this drama. There is absolutely nothing to do except witness this beautiful play of energy, these "Divine dances" of energies. Just witness this happening all around, in all relationships, and in all types of institutions crumbling at a rapid rate globally ~

We are all so fortunate to be alive right now ~ actively participating in this portal of 2012 ~ actively surrendering to the Divine Presence to fully take over our lives ~ when this happens, the shifts in consciousness brings swift and rapid clearings in all relationships, thus eventually bringing a freedom from the bondages of all relationships ~

Remembering that god consciousness literally IGNITES AND BURNS the ego within ourselves and others all around us brings the awareness to honor ourselves and others during this process. This journey of Awakening is truly for warriors ~ spiritual and galactic warriors on all levels ~

100

ABUNDANCE = GRACE

ABUNDANCE = GRACE
The Law of Abundance

The Law of Abundance states that the Universe is *infinitely* abundant. To access this infinite abundance, people must let Divine gifts flow to them and, more importantly, *through them*. This means: what comes in, *must* go out. What comes in *must* be shared, to keep the Universal flow of energy moving.

The minute one stops the flow of abundance out = the minute the Universe will stop its flow of abundance in, in direct ratio. Utilize what you "need," of course, then share the Divine gifts of abundance with others, especially those less fortunate than you. This generates much more abundance to flow to you and creates positive karma.

One must never "hoard" Divine gifts, for this actually is based on "fear" and blocks the flow of Divine Grace ~

The Law of Abundance pertains to ALL things:

- Money ~ finances and material wealth.
- Teachings ~ Universal truths and wisdom.
- Words ~ compliments, positive reinforcement.
- Gifts ~ a flower.
- Gestures ~ helping someone carry their groceries, helping people with disabilities.
- Thoughts and prayers.

- Love.
- AND DEEKSHA ~ helping facilitate Awakening and God-Realization. You have the most amazing Divine gift of Deeksha, literally at your fingertips; are you sharing this gift at *every given opportunity*?

The more you give in **ALL** areas of life, the more you receive. This is the very simple Universal Principle ~ start utilizing this premise today! If you desire wealth, then give money to others. If you desire Awakening, then actively help others on their Awakening journey. If you desire good health, then help others with their own health and healing.

Let's focus on material wealth. *All material wealth* = Divine Energy, which comes in ALL forms, especially in the form of finances.

So money = Divine Grace, Divine Gifts, and Divine intervention coming to us and "through" us to make our lives and other people's lives better ~

This **IS** Divine will. Until the shift of Awakening occurs, the sense of "I" creates stories of where success and wealth come from. Some of these stories are as follows:

- "I" created this wealth.
- "I" work hard.
- "I" am smart; "I" went to a good college, so now "I" am successful.
- "I" *achieved* all of this success.

True, maximum external effort is necessary for ANY SUCCESS in life. However, when the sense of "I" claims "responsibility" for the abundance through Grace, then these stories actually = *pure arrogance.*

Once the shifts of Awakening and God-Realization have occurred, the "I" is dissolved, and all that is left is the realization that god consciousness **IS** flowing through the physical "me," and this body *IS ONLY A VEHICLE FOR DIVINE GRACE.* The realization is that the Divine has "created ALL this" and has ever been able to "create ALL this." The arrogance shatters completely and it is transmuted into pure humility. This all happens naturally and is a progression within the Awakening process. Through no effort of our "own" can this be practiced or cultivated.

How can arrogance still exist when the experiential realization is that it is ALL "Divine Grace" flowing through? It simply cannot ~ Since the sense of "I" blocks Grace, once this is dissolved, then only pure Grace can flow through at maximum flow. You see, arrogance is the role of the "I"; how could it ever not be?

For example, the common story is "I have done all these great deeds in my life." Once the "I" (*thus arrogance)* is shattered, all that can remain is *pure humility.* And in fact, the greater success in one's life and the greater the "deeds," the GREATER the Divine's hand in one's life, which naturally brings greater humility! So you see, this humility sees abundance *AS* the Divine hand in one's life.

How many times do you say "NO" to abundance? Reflect on this for a moment . . . every time you say "NO" to abundance, you actually are saying "NO" to the Divine hand of Grace! How can it ever not be this way?

Abundance comes in so many different forms: wisdom, health, wealth, spiritual realizations (shifts of consciousness)

= Mind + Body + Spirit being ALL interconnected.

So when you say "NO" to material wealth (money and finances), you are actually saying "NO" to the Divine's gifts in ALL areas of life, for they are all connected. Grace is ALL around, to bestow infinite gifts on us ~ it is up to us to say "YES" to these gifts. In fact, the more we say "YES," the more the gifts are bestowed. This **IS** a basic principle of the Universe.

This relates to the complete importance of Awakening and God-Realization, for then there will no longer be a sense of "I" to block Divine Grace, and the individual realizes he **IS** a pure vehicle of Divine Grace, *of god's will here on the planet!* Then god consciousness **IS** flowing freely ~

Some may have the question: "It seems that so many people on the so-called spiritual path actually shun money and material wealth ~ can you explain this in detail?"

Answer: This is just a form of the "spiritual ego". Another "story of the I" is that to be spiritual, one must not seek money. This particular story of the "I" has given one the identity (conditioning and belief) that, "Look at me, I am *so* spiritual, because I shun money", when really this just = extreme separation from god and the Divine abundance of the Universe. This belief is an identity of the ego.

There are people, however, on the spiritual path who are truly not attached to money, so there is a definite distinction between *true* "non-attachment" to material wealth and gain versus actually "shunning" material wealth.

The Oneness University's vision is for individuals to be spiritual AND successful, at the same time. Not one or the other; a choice does not have to be made between these two things. In fact, quite the contrary ~ these two things are "inter"-connected with each other since the exact same Universal Laws are utilized to create success and wealth, as for spiritual growth and Awakening! For example, a very successful person already is in the flow of the Universal energies, so the same principles to attain material success can be utilized in one's spiritual life:

1.) Intention = Vision for oneself.
2.) Effort = Working incredibly hard and putting in maximum external effort = Law of Action.
3.) Grace is asked for and is the fuel for all growth and success ~ *Ask and you shall receive.*

These are true for success in ALL areas of life: Health, Wealth, Spiritual Growth, and Awakening.

The West is so focused materially; look how prosperous the Western world is, especially the United States. This means that, *in general,* people are utilizing the Universal Laws for material gain. This has, however, created an imbalance spiritually.

In contrast, in the East (in particular India), the traditions have been so focused on spiritual Awakening that there has been an imbalance materially. So what must happen now, and **IS** happening, is the merging of the Eastern and Western traditions (spiritual + material) to bring balance into people's lives, internally and externally, thus balancing the planet as a whole. Once people become more balanced internally, the external world will then automatically become more balanced. For example, environmental issues, disease, and poverty will all have solutions.

The first step is to just be AWARE if you are living a life of "abundance" or not ~ just SEE where you are with this.

Do you say "YES" to all the abundance the Universe regularly has to offer? Or do you regularly say "NO"? Just see ~ The next step is to ask for Grace's help, for Grace can and will bring all the gifts of the Universe to you, in the form of spiritual Awakening, wealth, and good health.

In closing, actively utilize the Law of Abundance! The more people on the planet actively and consciously engaging in "What comes in, must go out" will create more abundance for ALL living things! Greed, poverty, and disease would then not be able to exist, and Awakening would be accessible to all ~ Please remember, ALL Divine gifts MUST be shared, however great and small ~ Divine gifts must never be "hoarded," for this will stop the flow of the Universe coming in ~

101

WEALTH CONSCIOUSNESS IS GOD CONSCIOUSNESS ~

WEALTH CONSCIOUSNESS IS GOD CONSCIOUSNESS

Wealth Consciousness is NOT a destination ~ Just as God-Realization is a "Journey," so is Wealth Consciousness. And it is "all dependent" on your bond with the Divine; why? Because the Divine is bestowing ALL abundance to you, in so many forms:

- Love and Relationships ~
- Health and Healing ~
- Finances and Opportunities ~
- Universal Wisdoms, Truths, and Shifts in Consciousness ~

There is no difference between asking for Awakening and God-Realization and asking for Wealth Consciousness. So-called "differences" have been created by the sense of "I", with "stories," beliefs, and conditionings; some of these patterns stemming from lifetimes ago.

The sense of "I" loves the "STORY OF LACK"; why? Because anywhere lack exists, god cannot ~ It is as simple as that. So the sense of "I" drives this LACK CONSCIOUSNESS, as if it were a machine.

THE MORE LACK = THE LESS GOD

LACK CANNOT EXIST WHERE GOD CONSCIOUSNESS EXISTS~

ABUNDANCE = GOD

Right now, the "powers that be" on the planet know how to continually churn the "story of lack": through media-based outlets and the status quo. Of course, the human mind is powerful beyond belief, and the global elite know this, so they steer the collective consciousness deeper and deeper into "lack consciousness," which really = SEVERE SEPARATION FROM GOD.

So what is the way out of this for an individual? Focus on your bond with the Divine, with god, with the All That Is, with THE FIELD of Grace. The Universe is infinitely abundant ~ this will be an intellectual concept until the shifts of consciousness bring it as EXPERIENTIAL REALITY.

~ THE UNIVERSE IS "THE FIELD" OF GRACE ~

"THE FIELD" IS:

- GOD
- THE DIVINE
- THE INFINITELY ABUNDANT UNIVERSE
- WAITING TO BESTOW ABUNDANCE IN *ALL* AREAS OF YOUR LIFE

So the "Journey" of Wealth Consciousness **IS** the "Journey" of your bond with the Divine. Utilize all of the Deeksha processes, for these are the fastest way to journey with your Divine, to merge with your Divine ~

**Those seeking Wealth Consciousness must realize that
"Lack Consciousness" simply
= a severe separation from god ~**

The Deeksha Processes are bringing the shifts of consciousness where the Universe is accessible, in ALL areas of your life: Awakening, Realizing God, and Wealth Consciousness. That is why ALL the shifts of consciousness go hand-in-hand ~ they are ALL inter-connected ~

Individuals in the West NOW have the tools to access these shifts of consciousness and to access ALL the gifts of Abundance the Universe is ready to bestow.

~ EMPOWERMENT IS A CHOICE ~

TO BE "EMPOWERED"

= TO BE "IN POWER," WITH THE UNIVERSE

PLEASE REMEMBER:

ACCESSING ABUNDANCE

= TAKING ACTION ~

This **IS** absolutely necessary to realize your dreams and goals. The opposite of this = INACTION, which is really the same as laziness. The Universe responds to ACTION. This is a simple principle that MUST be utilized, constantly and consistently ~

102

THE NATURE OF FEAR ~

THE NATURE OF FEAR
The Universal Laws Intertwined

Fear is created by the "I," to block out all Divine Grace. Of course! This is how the "I" survives ~

This is one of mankind's greatest issues right now! Fear absolutely and completely blocks out growth and opportunity. Mankind, thus the "I," is too attached to "good experiences," and so very fearful of bad experiences.

THIS REALLY

= *FEARFUL OF LIVING, OF LIFE, AND OF EXPERIENCING DIVINE GRACE* ~

The "I" would rather not experience anything at all than experience anything labeled as "bad."

What can mankind do about this fear-based modality?

There is only one thing that can be done, that is for the Self to dissolve.

No Self

= Divine Presence Meeting Divine Presence ~
All experiences then

= meeting and "INTER"-acting with the Divine
Presence ~

Which

= "INTER"-acting with ALL life,

thus THE FIELD ~

This is strictly a psychological concept that the "I" cannot grasp,
ever ~ until there is no "I" or sense of "Self," that person will be
ruled by fear. Unfortunately, the "powers that be" of the planet
know how to manipulate the "I" of mankind and have it focus
on fear, which is really a very low vibration and energy. The
media and "powers that be" stoke the "I", "enliven" the "I" of
mankind. This is very easy to do. Once this engine is started, it
is very easy to lead. Most advertising and consumerism = based
on "*feeding the I.*"

Television and the various news sources are tools to generate fear
in the collective; TURN THEM OFF ~

The only way to combat fear = dissolve the "I." This **IS** freedom
from fear.

So why is it important to confront fears of the "I"? Why is this a
great spiritual sadhana (practice)?

Focusing on the deepest, darkest fears of the "I" = bringing in
"the light," exposing them. Without doing this, the fears reside in
the dark, hidden in the depths. These are the underlying currents
that run a person's life. By exposing them, the "I" SEES the fears
and "owns" them; then and only then can you ask the Divine
Presence to shatter these fears. Grace is the only thing powerful
enough to break open these fears. Ask for the Deeksha to explode
this fear pattern. All that remains is pure Presence.

So it is important for the "I" to take the time each and every day to examine his fears, write them down.

For example, what is your:

- Fear of Awakening?
- Fear of Money (lack of it or too much)?
- Fear of Relationships (being alone or of intimacy)?

With Deeksha and Divine Grace, the "I" will start to SEE the fears as being generated from past experiences, charges, even lifetimes ago.

It takes a tremendous amount of courage and Grace to continually exercise this type of self-introspection on a daily basis. Of course! This is why we are all here. There is only a very small percentage of people on the planet right now that can actually do this sadhana. These are the spiritual warriors! These are the ONES called to the Oneness Phenomenon; they have the courage. True, not everyone has the courage ~ Kalki's ONES do. They have the courage ~

After the shifts of Awakening and God-Realization, fear still arises and falls, of course! However, ONE SEES the fear as just that: a "thought-form to be experienced." There will no longer be attachment to fear; how could there be? The "I" has dissolved, and all that is left is pure Divine Presence experiencing pure Divine Presence ~

Postscript. There has been so much talk about specific "dates" and "events happening" these next few years, for example in movies and within spiritual groups. Should the public really be focusing on certain dates?

Of course not ~ Do not be concerned with dates. The need to focus on dates and future events is only generated by the sense of "I" ~ of course, because the "I" only seeks survival. This very easily turns into *FEAR*.

Fear and Distractions are very intertwined in today's modern world. These are actually very powerful tools designed to move a person "away from god". The more "separate from god", the more FEAR is able to take over. Fear is such a separating factor and is why the "powers that be" utilize it. There is no need to go on about this, since it is all based on the Universal Laws.

You can picture a downward spiral ~ this is how FEAR takes an individual down. LIKE ATTRACTS LIKE. This is all due to the principles of the Law of Resonance, the Law of Attraction, and the Law of Intention.

It is far more beneficial and necessary in this critical time in mankind's evolution to utilize these same Universal Laws to focus on a "higher vision" for the planet = *Oneness and "heaven on earth."*

Oneness and "heaven on earth" exist *within* the individual. Continue the spiritual practices (sadhanas) that bring the shifts of consciousness of *Oneness and "heaven on earth"* until these ARE your experiential reality. It IS happening NOW, the upward spiral of mankind's evolution into the higher vibration of ONENESS and God-Realization ~

103

2012-2014: THE YEARS OF UNPARALLED OPPORTUNITY FOR AWAKENING, GROWTH, AND TRANSFORMATION ~

This applies to ALL areas of one's life:

Spiritually ~ There is extraordinary access to Grace for growth in consciousness; for the shifts of Awakening; and for the bond with your god to grow exponentially. Of course! This is what the Oneness Phenomenon is all about. This is what everyone who has been working tirelessly for this grand window of opportunity has been waiting for! This is what everyone's hard work within the Oneness movement has been working up to ~ for this small window of extraordinary amounts of Grace descending into mankind.

This is because we are completing AND beginning a twenty-six-thousand-year cycle of mankind's evolution in consciousness. Let's just say an incredible "portal" is open these few years: for Grace, for the Divine, to descend fully and completely into man ~ It will not happen to everyone at this time. Actually, it will happen to only a very small percentage of the world's population. It has all been aligned eons ago as "sacred contracts," meaning it has already been written in your "records."

Those actively working with the Avataric consciousness of Oneness are the ONES Divinely aligned, of course ~

~ YOU ARE THE ONES ~

~ YOU WHO ARE READING THESE WORDS ~

~ YOU ARE THE ONES ALIGNED WITH ONENESS CONSCIOUSNESS ~

Utilize Deeksha and these processes as facilitators of them, as participants of them, for you are the VEHICLES OF THIS DIVINE Grace.

BECOME a Deeksha Giver ~

BECOME a Trainer ~

The tools of Awakening are literally in your hands ~

There is no "ONE" else, it is YOU ~

As well as spiritually, this same portal of 2012-2014 is granting ALL ACCESS to Abundance; Love and Relationships; Health and Healing. Of course! Because it is all the infinite access of god-consciousness, delivering all of these opportunities to you ~ it is not one or the other. You do not have to choose; it does not have to be Spiritual *or* Financially Abundant.

~ IT HAS ALWAYS BEEN BEING SPIRITUAL *AND* INFINITELY ABUNDANT ~

The Universe (THE FIELD of Grace) does not pick and choose to give you one thing BUT not the other ~ that doesn't make sense. It is mankind that makes this choice, unconsciously or consciously, all day, every day.

I say, make this choice CONSCIOUSLY ~

Say YES YES YES to an infinitely abundant Universe to bestow all the gifts of Grace to you:

- Spiritually ~
- Through Relationships + Love ~
- With Health + Healing ~

What the planet needs now are empowered individuals saying YES, loudly and clearly to the Universe, to be the spiritual warriors, the true "super soldiers of light," to be the ONES ~

So the question is, will you say YES? Will you be the ONE with infinite access to the Universe?

Remember, as we are in these very auspicious years of 2012–2014, you are exactly where you are meant to be, all as perfect preparation for the opportunities abounding this year! These years **ARE** extraordinary because of this unparalleled opportunity for awakening, growth, and transformation delivered by Grace~

104

THE QUICKENING =
THE ACCELERATED TIMES
OF DIVINE GRACE

THE QUICKENING = THE ACCELERATED TIMES OF DIVINE GRACE
The Law of Abundance

We are in the times of the "the quickening" of our dreams and intentions manifesting. This includes ALL dreams of abundance, love, friendships, community, awakenings, and realizing god.

Focus your attention and intention on "the quickening" of manifesting your dreams and goals in all sectors of your life:

- ABUNDANCE OF FINANCES AND WEALTH ~
- HEALTH AND HEALING ~
- RELATIONSHIPS OF LOVE AND FRIENDSHIPS ~

Yes, the time is NOW to access the infinite abundance the Universe has to bestow on us. No one is to be left behind ~ NOW is the time to actively utilize the Law of Abundance to bring the flow of the Universe to you and, more importantly, *THROUGH YOU*. You see, the times are such right NOW, and in these coming years, that *instant manifestation* is here. When utilizing this Law of Abundance properly:

THE MORE YOU GIVE

= THE MORE YOU RECEIVE

~ BECAUSE THE UNIVERSE IS INFINITELY ABUNDANT ~

In addition to manifesting abundance, dreams and goals are also being realized through the Universal Law of Attraction. This means:

You think it

= You live it

= Your Experiential Reality ~

So it does take extreme personal responsibility, *thus empowerment*, to focus on the positive ways to manifest. Are you tied to "prophecies," news stories, "worst-case scenarios"? If so, and no judgment here, just refocus this to the much more positive outcome of "BEST-CASE SCENARIOS." It is wisest not to watch these types of news commentaries and media outlets, as a lot of them are designed to generate fear, especially using images that get etched in your mind. This is a very well thought out plan to keep mankind, thus the planet, gripped in fear.

MOVING TOWARD FEAR

= MOVING AWAY FROM GOD ~

FEAR

= THE ABSENCE OF GOD ~

GOD

= THE ABSENCE OF FEAR ~

~ It is as simple as that ~

Mother Earth is giving birth right now, to the higher consciousness of Oneness. This outer manifestation of "THE SHIFT" is necessary for the INNER SHIFT to occur. The two are dependent on each other; one cannot happen without the other.

THIS OUTER SHIFT = DIVINE WILL

As more and more people "realize" this through shifts in consciousness, the less the outer manifestations occur, thus the importance of Awakening and realizing god.

Focus on "the quickening" of:

- LOVE
- FRIENDSHIPS
- COMMUNITY
- HEALTH AND HEALING
- AWAKENING
- REALIZING GOD
- CONTRIBUTION

You see, these Divine Energies are available NOW for the quickening of ALL things ~

Utilize these energies properly; it **IS** our responsibility to do so~

Every minute of every day, we have choices to be made.

Do we choose Love, Oneness, and Realizing GOD?

Or

Do we choose Fear, Hopelessness, and Despair?

You see, fear has the capacity to completely "paralyze" an individual, to stop you in your tracks on your awakening journey. Fear is such a great hindrance to these shifts of Awakening and God-Realization.

There is such a simple sadhana (spiritual practice). When you find yourself "stuck in fear," simply:

1.) Sit with this fear.
2.) Recognize it.
3.) Surrender to it, and call out to your Divine.
4.) Take a powerful Deeksha and ASK your Divine for the fear to be dissolved completely and immediately. Try this in the evening and before going to bed. The Universe will respond and miracles will happen to you. You just might find that when you wake up, the fear has indeed been dissolved completely! Try it for yourself and see what happens. The more you utilize the Divine for your growth, the more the Divine responds with instant responses to your needs. It is exquisite, and this is the very nature of how the Divine works ~

~ GROWTH CANNOT HAPPEN WITHOUT THE DIVINE ~

In closing, it is critical that mankind remembers EMPOWERMENT, and that each and every choice we make does matter ~ Please remember to utilize these "quickening" times and Divine energies to manifest *infinite* abundance, love, friendships, community, and health. Please remind others to do the same; what the planet needs now are individuals constantly and consistently choosing the PATH OF LOVE over fear ~

105

EARTH CHANGES ~

EARTH CHANGES
Law of Allowance

Earth Changes signify *outer shifting* + *inner shifting*. The planet has already been experiencing Earth Changes and will keep experiencing them throughout the coming years. This is a re-shifting of energies, a realigning of the global energies. So much is happening everywhere ~ Be prepared; enjoy being at home with your family.

Utilize the *Law of Allowance*, which states, "Allow things to happen around you." This = the natural progression of events. The *allowance* of people, places, and things to cycle and complete their journeys and lessons. This all = Divine Order. The greatest thing man can do is "allow" the natural course of the cycle of events and happenings. God will guide you when to intervene, and when to allow.

The Law of Allowance automatically turns into "acceptance" of situations, people, and events. The opposite of this creates "resistance," and what we resist . . . persists. Allowing the "natural" progression of events is actually very freeing and relieving! The "controller" no longer has a job. This "controller" is the sense of "I."

Once Awakened and God-Realized, the individual lives within alignment of the Law of Allowance, which becomes an "effortless" life where "all things are happening automatically." You see, the

"I" creates a sense of "control" over one's life, situations, and other people.

This = the greatest falsehood and illusion ~

The cosmic joke is that the "I" tries to have control . . . control over what? The Universe? God? Divine Will? Now this is truly a laughable cosmic joke and a delusion. Trying to "have control" over anything actually works against all Universal Spiritual Laws and creates incoherence, disharmony. This goes against the "true nature" of the Universe and creates havoc on the planet. It is far wiser to SEE this grand paradox! The unawakened one can "know" this illusion as an intellectual concept. The awakened one is dissolved of this illusion = freedom.

So again, this brings us back to the *importance* of Awakening and God-Realization. The more Awakened and God-Realized beings walking the planet, the greater "coherence" created for mankind as a whole, which thus creates greater coherence with all life and creatures.

THIS = LIVING IN ONENESS

In closing, the outer + inner shifting are necessary. THE SHIFT **IS** happening. It **IS** god's will, it **IS** the Divine plan. The more people actively participating in awakening and the oneness work worldwide, the greater global coherence for ALL!

106

PARADIGM SHIFT: THE NEED TO CONTROL AND OWN VS. THE REFUSAL TO BE CONTROLLED AND OWNED ~

PARADIGM SHIFT: THE NEED TO CONTROL AND OWN VS. THE REFUSAL TO BE CONTROLLED AND OWNED

THE OLD PARADIGM PATTERNS = THE CONDITIONINGS AND THE MENTAL PROGRAMMING PATTERNS OF THE NEED TO:

- Control
- Own
- Manipulate
- Exert Power Over Others

= A long-standing one indeed, spanning thousands and thousands of years of Earth's history. The reason "why" and "how" it started is not necessary to explain here ~ all that is needed is to SEE this "conditioning" playing out in human drama, and that it is ending, very abruptly, right now ~ as the suppressed goddess energy is emerging through humans and various institutions across the planet

~ It is emerging in a strong upward movement and affecting everyone and everything it touches =

THE CRUMBLING OF INSTITUTIONS AND RELATIONSHIPS BASED ON THE OLD PARADIGM ~

No longer can the ego games of manipulation, control, or "sense of ownership" be sustained ~ the "new earth" based on "heaven on earth" is being birthed right now, through the goddess energies, the Divine feminine, as higher states of consciousness reveal all these ancient patterns being perpetuated on planet Earth.

All this is a "balancing act" for the masculine energies that have prevailed in a gross imbalance of energies ~ this **IS** all being balanced out now.

ENERGY GAMES = EGO GAMES

"SEE" it in your own relationships:

1.) How is the old paradigm crumbling in your current relationships?
2.) Where are manipulation, control, and sense of ownership rapidly crumbling (sometimes in uncomfortable ways) as the new energies of the Divine feminine are emerging?
3.) How is this affecting your loved ones?
4.) How is this affecting all your relationships, including business partnerships?
5.) How is this affecting you?
6.) Are you SEE-ing very clearly YOUR ROLE in this human drama?
7.) Do you SEE how you attracted this, through the Law of Resonance, into your life? Are you playing the role of "refusing to be dominated" or "to be someone else's property"?

Just SEE your role in perpetuating this OLD paradigm ~

And more importantly, SEE how your role is to now SHIFT this paradigm, through your very own SHIFTS OF CONSCIOUSNESS ~ SEE how Grace is shifting these paradigms swiftly and rapidly within yourself, your loved ones, and institutions around the planet.

YES ~ Grace is creating this NEW EARTH, right before our eyes! Yes, it is happening rapidly ~ we are here on planet Earth during these great years of 2012-2014 to SHIFT these paradigms:

1.) The Need to Control/Manipulate/Own

2.) Refusing to be Controlled/Manipulated/Owned

You see, these two "roles" (conditionings) attract each other, thus the reason for the thousands of years of this human drama ~ It **IS** all crumbling right now; the energies of this portal of 2012-2014 are swiftly igniting these shifts in human consciousness ~ How lucky are we to witness this as the "observer" and allow these illusions of the collective ego to be revealed in such a grand and powerful way?

WHAT REMAINS IS TRUE FREEDOM = LIBERATION

~ LIBERATION FROM THE BONDAGES OF ALL RELATIONSHIPS ~

Praise your Divine each and every day for this swift acting Grace that is bringing us these shifts this year ~ for it all must be given thanks and praise!

~ THIS IS A DIVINE-LED ODYSSEY ~

~ All ONE simply needs is a shift of consciousness to REALIZE this ~

107

WHAT IS ENERGY MANAGEMENT?

WHAT IS ENERGY MANAGEMENT?

ENERGY MANAGEMENT = EMPOWERMENT

EMPOWERMENT

= "IN POWER"

= AT ONE WITH THE UNIVERSE

"Lack of empowerment" is simply a conditioning, a fear, perhaps from many lifetimes, perhaps spanning thousands of years. This conditioning stops individuals dead in their tracks. Actually this "fear" has been projected on mankind for thousands of years; why? To make an incredibly subservient race of humans, of course!

Ah, how we have "played" into this role ~ we actually took on the "sacred contract" to be controlled, to be manipulated, to be owned.

But no longer can these "energy games" exist; why? Because of the great shift of the ages, the window of enormous amounts of Grace are accessible to all, to WAKE UP, to SEE these paradigms, being played on planet Earth, to REALIZE our own roles in perpetuating this paradigm, this ancient "agenda."

~ GRACE IS HERE NOW ~

~ TO BREAK UP THESE PARADIGMS FOREVER ~

Only Grace has the power to do this; how? Through "inner transformation," of ourselves, of course. Inner transformation will = outer transformation. We cannot change the "outer" without first transforming the "inner"~ This is one of the biggest illusions, that there is an "I" who can control the outer enough to "change" it. Once this fallacy is realized, all that is left is Divine Grace, readily accessible to transform the inner. Once we SURRENDER to the infinite FIELD of Grace, once we consciously ask for this, only then will Grace DELIVER ~

Test it, try it right now ~ Look very deeply into your own life, and especially within your relationships, whether it is with:

- A Partner
- Parents, Siblings, Children
- Friends
- Business Partnerships

"SEE" THE PARADIGMS BEING PLAYED OUT:

- The NEED TO CONTROL, through manipulation, sense of ownership, and "power over" the other.
- "ALLOW"-ing to be controlled, having a "lack of power" to say NO to this.
- REFUSING to be controlled, manipulated, owned.

Just SEE how these are playing out in your life right now ~

Now SEE how these roles are being perpetuated on a grand scale throughout the planet.

How "tangled" up in them are you? If you are sensitive, you can feel these ENERGY ENTANGLEMENTS:

1.) Physically ~ for example, around your heart, your solar plexus, and various other areas that correlate with the chakra system
2.) Within your various energy body and auric field

Only Grace can untangle this for us ~ what is needed first are the "realizations" = the SEE-ing of all that is going on with others and ourselves ~ and realizing we "attract" all these energy dynamics. We must now say YES to Grace, to growth, and to transformations so that these energy games can be released forever, personally and collectively.

Please remember, empowerment is our choice ~ Do you want to be FREE, from lifetimes of "energy bondages"? If your answer is yes, Divine Grace is here to deliver. The power of Deeksha and the Oneness processes are such that during these years of 2012-2014, infinite possibilities exist:

1.) To Realize our own roles in these manipulation games ~
2.) To Break these bondages forever ~
3.) To Realize the Divine hand in everything ~
4.) To Fully surrender to Divine Grace ~

So the question is, do you say YES to this?

108

THERE ARE NO "MAYBES" WITH THE UNIVERSE ~

THERE ARE NO "MAYBES" WITH THE UNIVERSE

~ Say YES or NO to THE FIELD of Grace, loudly and clearly ~

YOU ARE EITHER:

MOVING FORWARD →

OR

← MOVING BACKWARD

Anytime you have an intention, a "vision," you must take the appropriate steps to move forward, even if they are small, baby steps.

Each baby step forward = a proclamation to the Universe, which says: "YES, I say YES to this intention, to this dream, to this vision" ~

THE UNIVERSE OPERATES ON YESSES AND NOS ~

THERE ARE NO "MAYBES" WITH THE UNIVERSE ~

The Universe, THIS FIELD of Grace, absolutely requires a firm YES, for you to move forward with your intention → to set the energies "in motion"

OR

A firm NO to cut "all energies" and to stop the energetic "play."

A NO is absolutely necessary to stop all the creative forces of the Universe that were originally put into motion. You are so powerful; empower yourself right NOW with this energetic play. You will swiftly cut through all the noxious weeds, which **IS** the path of empowerment ~

What exactly are you "wishing" of yourself right now? What are you intending? What are you visioning? Pick one of your specific desires/projects/outcomes ~ Now bring it fully into your awareness, and with the desired outcome ~ Sit with this for a few moments, "feel" inside your body. Now I ask you the question: Have you said a YES, loudly and clearly, to the desired outcome? This is where inner integrity comes into play ~ What is your honest answer to this question? How does your body feel? Where is there tightness felt? Where are blockages or fears or resistance felt? Scan your body: are any of these felt in your heart? Your solar plexus? Your throat? Other areas?

If you truly have not said YES, there is absolutely no way the Universe can bring the desired outcome into fruition; why? Because it **IS** up to you to take the appropriate steps forward:

→ TO YOUR DESIRED OUTCOME ~

This is based on the LAW OF ACTION = Taking the necessary external effort on your part as a human being to fulfill your desired wishes and outcomes. When you took the "sacred contract" to take human form, you agreed to certain Spiritual Laws of the Universe to be co-creators on planet earth.

LIVING = CO-CREATING ~

OTHERWISE, WHAT IS THE PURPOSE OF LIFE?

The purpose of life is to:

GROW, TO TAKE STEPS FORWARD, NO MATTER HOW GREAT

OR SMALL

→ TO CO-CREATE WITH THE UNIVERSAL FIELD OF GRACE.

IN FACT ALL SPIRITUAL LAWS ARE AT OUR FINGERTIPS, TO UTILIZE, AS CO-CREATORS ~

We are simply vehicles of Divine Grace ~ with these spiritual Laws to EMPOWER us to bring us to our highest potential.

~ SAYING YES IS THE ENERGETIC SIGNATURE OF THE CO-CREATIVE HUMAN ~

"SEE" now in your own life, where you say "maybes" ~

MAYBES = NON-ACTION, NON-CREATING

To manifest anything in life takes a strong YES! This is the most important word in the creative Universe; of course NO is equally as powerful and important, for

NO = THE ENERGETIC STOP TO ALL CREATIVE FORCES

Have you been able to say "NO," loudly and firmly, to people, situations, events, even places that you have no desire of having energetic ties with? Or is there a "FEAR" or "CONDITIONING" that speaking this "NO" will upset someone, cause offense, or start a confrontation?

You must understand, an EMPOWERED person must say YES → TO DESIRED OUTCOMES

AND

NO → To a person, place, or thing not aligned with their desired outcomes ~

EMPOWERMENT = "TAKING A CLEAR STANCE" ONE WAY OR THE OTHER

~ REMEMBER, THERE ARE NO "MAYBES" WITH THE UNIVERSE ~

When there are deep-seated FEARS stopping you from saying "YES" and "NO," realize these can be from so many different lifetimes ~ This is where Grace is absolutely necessary to smash these fears to pieces ~ take a very powerful Deeksha, with the specific intention to "dissolve this fear" immediately ~

GRACE WILL DELIVER ~

MIRACLES WILL HAPPEN ~

THIS IS GUARANTEED ~

The sooner you start to say firm YESSES and NOS, the sooner the Universe will respond accordingly with all of your desired outcomes ~

EPILOGUE

Dying to Drink from the Eternal Cup of Grace
Devotional writing to my Divine ~

Oh my beloved, I praise you for this love affair with you, which only you could have bestowed on me. How could I have spent my whole life without you? It was sheer torture, not to know you, sheer loneliness and separation, a life of madness within the mind. My beloved, I was your lost child, child of god. Thrown out into this world as an orphan. Homesick for you, the all-encompassing love of my life, the only thing worth living for. All the years, all the roads traveled, all the miles traversed ~ simply to be reunited with you, my beloved, my master, my holy love affair with you, the Divine. Every cell now filled with your infinite Grace, ALIVE with Grace, light, and LIFE ~

I praise you for this exquisite existence, this exquisite shift you bestowed to me, to realize you, this bond, and discovery of you ~ of my master, my Divine teacher, my holy beloved ~ This "new" existence has been exquisite indeed, paradise lost is now paradise found ~ This IS heaven on earth. This is heaven AS earth ~ heaven is earth, and earth is heaven. To BE this vehicle of Grace IS heaven on earth. This physical body IS the god-link between heaven and earth, as the vehicle of pure Grace ~

My god, my love, how did I ever survive without you before? Of course, I didn't. I was dying, a slow and miserable death of loneliness, of separation. Death was "the me," for there was no life ~ only Grace brings life. Every cell was dying, dying to drink from the eternal cup of Grace. Only god's Grace fills this cup with the eternal energy of bliss,

*joy, ecstasy, fulfillment, meaning ~ no amount of material wealth,
friends, or status quo could ever fill up the bottomless void that only you
could, my god, my beloved ~*

*God's Grace runs through me as a freight train of Divine energies, of
Avataric consciousness, of oneness. The hand of god has picked me up
and ascended me into the heavens, in the home of the gods, the all that
is, one of infinite possibilities, merging heaven and earth. I surrender,
I succumb, I allow, I accept all of your Grace to propel me forward in
an inferno of momentum, of infinite possibilities, realizing my highest
potential as a human being, right here, right now, during this great shift
of the ages, in a world of plenty for all ~*

*I am yours, do with me what you will, all for the Awakening of the
planet, one of infinite god consciousness pervading all, and a world of
abundance and plenty for all creatures great and small ~*

*I suckle at your tender love, your infinite power, and the gifts of Grace
you continually bestow to me. Your Grace flows to me and ultimately
through me. There is no thing, nor no one, more important and all
encompassing than this love affair with you, my beloved. A Grace-
filled life is a Grace-led life, and it is the only life worth living. I praise
you for this field of Grace, so accessible, so responsive, so tangible, so
generous, so at one ~*

*I praise you as the lover and beloved become ONE, as the master and
servant merge in holy matrimony, and as the sacred cosmic consciousness
flows through each and every cell of my being in an explosion of
Avataric light, BE-ing this beacon, this super soldier of light~*

I am eternally yours ~ do with me what you will ~

~ GRATITUDE ~

I express my enormous praise and gratitude to everyone who pushed me into bringing these "writings" to the public. You know you who you are: my cosmic brother ~ my sisters in oneness ~ You are truly my Divine angels. Without you, these "writings" would have remained in my notebooks, sitting in some desk drawers at home. We are all in this Divine dance of Oneness together, and I am so very grateful for each of you ~

I especially give thanks to my husband Adam who has stood by my side and grounded me to have made "all this" possible~

ADDENDUM

INFORMATION ABOUT THE
ONENESS UNIVERSITY IN INDIA

Taken with permission from www.OnenessUniversity.org:

WHAT IS ONENESS?

What is this World Changing Phenomenon that is helping people of all faiths and paths move into higher states of consciousness?

There is an amazing world changing Phenomena that is occurring to humanity at this time. Over one hundred million people across the planet are experiencing this Divine Phenomenon known as Deeksha which starts a profound process of spiritual awakening in a person.

Oneness University is the birthplace of this Divine Phenomenon; and is helping millions of people move into higher states of consciousness.

Oneness offers courses and programs throughout the world to help people from all paths, faiths, and walks of life to grow into the natural state a human being is built to be in, a state that is one with all that is.

Oneness exists to set humanity totally and unconditionally free. Oneness, a spiritual organization founded by Sri Amma and Sri Bhagavan, seeks to alleviate human suffering at its roots by awakening humanity into oneness, wherein every individual feels connected to all that is. The central understanding of Oneness is that inner transformation and awakening into higher states of consciousness is not an outcome of a mere intellectual understanding but a neurobiological process in the brain, whereby one's experience of life is redefined at its core. This is achieved by Oneness Deeksha, which is a process of transfer of Divine Grace that initiates a journey into higher states of consciousness.

The Deeksha is believed to affect the different lobes of the physical brain, thereby reducing stress levels and intensifying the levels of love, joy, and awareness. Millions across the globe testify the calming and awakening effects of the Oneness Deeksha, which is now slowly gaining recognition as by far the easiest and most effective approach to enriching human consciousness.

Settled majestically at the foothills of the Vellikonda range on the eastern coast of South India, 80km north of the city of Chennai, lies the Oneness University. A center for learning and growth, the Oneness University creates an atmosphere for people to learn and grow in consciousness leading to a "happy" individual and family. Catering to people of every faith and all walks of life, the University represents growth and learning in both the internal and the external spheres of life.

Oneness in many regards has a highly scientific approach, quite evident in many of Sri Amma Bhagavan's teachings and this actually comes as a relief to the many Oneness followers ranging from the younger generation and the intellectual/elite classes, who abhor blind belief and unscientific philosophy at all levels.

This kind of a vastly liberal and truly secular approach could be attributed to a very unique perception of Oneness that the founders Sri Amma and Sri Bhagavan share, who emphasize the beauty and importance of religious and cultural variety as every human being is unique and cannot discover his true self through one single path. It is therefore their message to the world that Oneness is not necessarily about making everyone embrace the same system of belief, doctrine or tradition but more a process of discovering the truth that is inherent in every tradition. Oneness as a concept is beautiful, as an experience is staggering.

Please visit: www.OnenessUniversity.org for more information on how to visit the campus and the Oneness Temple, and on how to enroll in the Oneness Processes offered there. Visit www.OnenessUsa.org to learn about Oneness in North America.